IN THE FIELD, ON THE COURT, AND ON THE RUN,
THE EXPERTS SWEAR BY *THE ATHLETE'S KITCHEN*

"Not only can a world-class athlete learn a lot from *The Athlete's Kitchen*, but it is great for anyone who is serious about improving their health. It has certainly helped me a great deal."
　　　　　　—Patti Catalano, American Women's Marathon
　　　　　　　Record Holder, 1980

"Athletes, in tuning their bodies finer and finer, want help in knowing how best to fuel their 'machines' to enhance maximum efficiency. Thanks to Nancy Clark, *now* we have it!"
　　　　　　—Tenley E. Albright, M.D., First American
　　　　　　　Women's Olympic and World Gold Medal
　　　　　　　Figure Skater

GO TO THE ENERGY SOURCE!
PEAK ATHLETIC PERFORMANCE BEGINS IN
THE ATHLETE'S KITCHEN!

THE ATHLETE'S KITCHEN

A Nutrition Guide and Cookbook

by Nancy Clark, M.S., R.D.
Nutritionist
Sports Medicine Resource, Inc.
Boston, Mass.

Illustrations by David Bastille

BANTAM BOOKS
TORONTO · NEW YORK · LONDON · SYDNEY · AUCKLAND

THE ATHLETE'S KITCHEN

*A Bantam Book / published by arrangement with
CBI Books*

PRINTING HISTORY
CBI edition published May 1981

Bantam edition / May 1983
2nd printing .... June 1984
3rd printing .... March 1986

Illustrations by David Bastille

ISBN 0-553-26117-7

Published simultaneously in the United States and Canada

PRINTED IN THE UNITED STATES OF AMERICA

O   12 11 10 9 8 7 6 5 4

Contents

Foreword

Like many of you who should read and profit from this book,
I'm a professional, a participant and a procrastinator.

As a professional in our multi-disciplined sportsmedicine
practice, I daily witness physical "problems" that can be
traced to inadequate understanding or utilization of proper
nutrition. As a runner and occasional marathoner, I've been
acutely aware of the proper and improper use of food as it
relates to athletic performance. As a procrastinator, living
a hectic life and having to eat on-the-run, I know I haven't
always sought the best nutritional education that would
allow me to make wiser food choices.

Nancy Clark has contributed much to our patients'
needs. Now she has managed to write as she performs—in a
delightfully breezy and down-to-earth authoritative style.
Here is one "cookbook" you'll find irresistible and irreplaceable.

Rob Roy McGregor, D.P.M.
Podiatrist, Sports Medicine Resource, Inc.
Boston, Massachusetts

ACKNOWLEDGMENTS

With sincere thanks and appreciation to:

Marshall Hoffman, for his continual encouragement.

David Bastille, for his patience and perseverance.

Janice Clark, for typing the manuscript.

Linda Piette and Ann Pitcher, for their recipes and
professional help.

My patients, for teaching me and sharing their experiences.

Donni Richman and Tim Baehr, for their assistance
in production.

Drs. William Southmayd, Rob Roy McGregor, and
William Shea, for their support.

I am grateful to those who contributed recipes:

Deborah Allen	Anne Hale	Nancy Mintz
David Bastille	Charles Healy	Alan Nowick
Carol Batrus	Shirley Huber	Gail Perrin
Joan Betterley	Maxine Hunter	Linda Piette
Debbie Clark	Lee Johnson	Ann Pitcher
Janice Clark	Vanessa Kearny	Gina Sanders
Liz Cunningham	Kim Kosciusko	Diane Sinski
Linda Ferraresso	Susan Krill	Barbara Volkle
Tim Gabriel	Carol Martin	Joanne Zitek
Paul Grady	Sandy Miller	

THE ATHLETE'S KITCHEN

Chapter 1

Sports Nutrition: The Science of Eating for Success

I am one of the few sports nutritionists in the United States. My job is to counsel both professional and recreational athletes in ways to get the most out of their diets. I am a registered dietitian who trained at the Massachusetts General Hospital. I received my Master's degree at Boston University, where I combined studies of nutrition with exercise physiology. In addition to my education, I have learned the importance of sports nutrition from personal experience. In 1978, I led 15 cyclists on a Trans-America 4,473-mile bicycle tour. I have also cycled extensively in the Canadian and Colorado Rocky Mountains. Because of my training and interest in sports, I am often asked questions such as:

- Should I take vitamin pills?
- Will junk food hurt my performance?
- What should I eat before competition?
- What is my ideal weight?

The majority of the patients I counsel worry about what they eat. "I don't have time to eat right," is their most common complaint. They want to know how to eat healthfully while on the run, and how to cook simple nutritious meals. For the most part, my patients are insecure about the quality of their diets. In my six years of practice, I have found that they have good reason to be.

Food is important for your general health and your athletic performance. As long as you get the forty basic nutrients and sufficient calories you will perform well. I don't have a magic diet for my patients or for you. "Metabolic magic" does not exist. Promises by health-food promoters about vitamin, protein and quick-energy supplements, crash diets, and fluid replacements are mainly hokum. I educate my patients with nutrition information based on scientific fact, rather than on hope. Competitive athletes have sport-specific nutritional needs. I translate the latest research by nutritionists and exercise physiologists into useful information. I recommend specific foods and eating patterns that will contribute to your optimal performance.

Marathoners ask, "Should I carbohydrate-load with fruits or pasta?" High school football players want to know,

"How can I gain weight that's muscle, but not fat?" Basketball players wonder, "What's the best fluid replacement?"

The purpose of this book is to correct the misinformation regarding sports nutrition and to help you select foods and prepare simple meals that will contribute toward top performance, as well as optimal health. Professional athletes and weekend exercisers alike will find the answers to these and other questions:

- What's good for an eat-on-the-run lunch that won't interfere with my afternoon workout?
- As a vegetarian weight-lifter, do I need protein supplements or vitamin pills?
- Is bread more effective than fruit for carbohydrate-loading?
- Are fresh vegetables nutritionally superior to frozen ones?
- Due to my training schedule, I eat heavily at night. Does this food turn to fat?
- Does coffee improve endurance performance?
- How nutritious is beer?

This "how-to" book will teach you to improve your daily training diet by shopping for healthful foods, preparing nutritious meals, and wisely choosing eat-on-the-run snacks. You'll also learn sport-specific tips, such as eating for the marathon and drinking to beat the heat on the tennis court. I recognize that knowing what is good for you doesn't necessarily mean that you will implement the information. But at least you will know the options. Here's to your health!

Chapter 2

How Do You Rate Your Diet?

Is Balancing Your Diet a Juggling Act?

Does a taste of guilt accompany your coffee-break-breakfast, vending-machine lunch, and eat-on-the-run dinner? Although busy runners may be too rushed to plan and prepare meals, "No time" is no excuse for a less than healthful diet. In the pages ahead you'll learn to become an expert on quick and easy nutrition. If you run for your health you should eat for your health. Good nutrition today

Guide to Good Eating: A Recommended Daily Pattern

The recommended daily pattern provides the foundation for a nutritious, healthful diet.

The recommended servings from the four food groups for adults supply about 1200–1500 calories. The chart below gives recommendations for the number and size of servings for several categories of people.

Food Group	Recommended Number of Servings			
	Child	Teenager	Adult	Pregnant Woman
Milk	3	4	2	4
1 cup milk, yogurt 1½ slices (1½ oz.) cheddar cheese 1 cup pudding 1¾ cups ice cream 2 cups cottage cheese				
Meat	2	2	2	3
2 ounces cooked, lean meat, fish, poultry 2 eggs 2 slices (2 oz.) cheddar cheese 1 cup dried beans, peas 4 tbsp. peanut butter				
Fruit-Vegetable	4	4	4	4
½ cup cooked or juice 1 cup raw (average piece fresh fruit)				
Grain (whole grain, fortified, enriched)	4	4	4	4
1 slice bread 1 cup ready-to-eat cereal ½ cup cooked cereal, pasta				

Courtesy: National Dairy Council.

The Basic Four Food Groups

Milk products provide:
calcium
riboflavin (B₂)
protein

Meat, fish, poultry, nuts, dried beans and peas provide:
protein
iron
zinc

Fruits and vegetables provide:
vitamin A
vitamin C

Bread, cereal, and grain products provide:
carbohydrates
thiamin (B₁)
iron
niacin
fiber

Foods are classified according to the vitamins and minerals they have. By eating a variety of different foods from the groups, you will get a variety of the nutrients you need for optimal health and performance.

is cheaper and easier to cope with than tomorrow's ailments.

To balance your diet, simply THINK before you eat. Are you choosing wholesome, basic foods, such as yogurt, apple, bran muffin, peanuts or grabbing for greasy, sugary foods, such as a jelly donut, chocolate bar, cup cake, or soda? If you choose wisely, in the course of the day you'll accumulate the nutrients you need. Eating three meals a day is not a criterion for a well-balanced diet. The total day's intake tells that story. How do you know if you are eating a "well-balanced" diet? The following recommended guide will give you the answer:

- Have you had TWO servings of dairy products? —perhaps milk on your cereal and yogurt for a snack—or cheese on your hamburger and a dish of ice cream?

- Have you had TWO small (2-ounce) servings of protein foods—peanut butter on your English muffin and a tuna sandwich? One 4-ounce (quarter-pounder) hamburger will suffice for the entire day's needs. Cheese on the pizza counts toward your protein intake only if in addition to the two milk group servings.

- Have you had fruit, juice, or vegetables FOUR times—a small (6-ounce) glass of orange juice at breakfast (a larger glass would count for two servings); a small apple at lunch; and later, a pizza with green peppers, mushrooms, and onions in addition to the tomato sauce?

- Have you had FOUR servings of breads, cereals, and grain products—a small bowl of cereal, a sandwich made with two slices of whole wheat bread, and a handful of rye crackers? *Enriched* whole-grain carbohydrates have more B-vitamins and iron than "natural," additive-free foods; they are a better choice for athletes. B-vitamins help

The Fundamental Forty Nutrients

1   Water

1   Carbohydrates

9   Protein: 9 essential amino acids:

     histidine   phenylalanine
     isoleucine   threonine
     leucine   tryptophan
     lysine   valine
     methionine

1   Fat: 1 essential fatty acid:

     linoleic acid

3   Electrolytes:

     sodium
     potassium
     chloride

13   Vitamins: 4 fat-soluble:
     A, D, E, K

     Vitamins: 9 water-soluble:

     B_1 (thiamin)   folacin
     B_2 (riboflavin)   biotin
     B_6 (pyridoxine)   pantothenic acid
     niacin   C (ascorbic acid)
     B_{12}

12   Minerals: 3 major:

     calcium
     phosphorous
     magnesium

     Minerals: 9 trace:

     iron   flouride
     zinc   chromium
     iodine   selenium
     copper   molybdenum
     manganese

40 Total

Other substances which are presently being studied to determine possible human requirements are:

aluminum	nickel
arsenic	silicon
boron	strontium
cadmium	titanium
choline	tin
cobalt	vanadium

By eating a variety of foods within the 2-2-4-4 food plan, you will get the fundamental forty nutrients required by the body to maintain good health.

Source: *Recommended Dietary Allowances*. National Research Council, National Academy of Sciences, Washington, D.C., 1980.

to convert the food you eat into energy for your muscles. Iron transports energy-producing oxygen to the muscles. Without B-vitamins and iron you'll be slow and tire easily.

Eat this 2-2-4-4 way to meet the recommended daily allowance for protein, vitamins, and minerals, except possibly for iron. [You'll learn how to solve the iron problem in the chapter on Bread.] You will need more calories, however. The 2-2-4-4 plan provides 1200-1500 calories—a nutritionally safe reducing diet for most people. Athletes eat more than 1500 calories, so add another 1000 or more for women and 1500 or more for men. If you would enjoy chomping these calories from potato chips, soda, and candy bars, you can and still be nutritionally safe. You will not develop deficiency diseases. You also will not promote your health. Junk foods do not improve your performance. Sugary and greasy foods supply lots of calories for fuel, but they lack the vitamins, minerals, and protein that your muscles need to function optimally. You fill your car with gasoline, but it still needs spark plugs to run. Similarly, when you fill your body with calories, remember that it needs nutrients to function well.

I recommend that you get the extra calories from the fruit, vegetable, and grain food groups. These foods are high

in carbohydrates and nutrients and are the best fuel for your muscles. Eat protein foods in moderation. Juicy meats are loaded with cholesterol and saturated fat. They are also more difficult to digest than carbohydrates, and contribute to heart disease.

When choosing your food, keep in mind the three keys to healthful eating:

1. **Variety.** There is no one magic food. Eat several

types of foods. Each will offer you different nutrients. If variety is a problem because you live alone, make a point of inviting someone to dinner once or twice a week. Not only will you eat better, you'll also enjoy the company.

2. Moderation. Your body may need less than your mind thinks it deserves. Don't get weighed down by the diseases of excess: obesity, diabetes, heart disease. Even athletes have to watch their weight.

3. Wholesomeness. Choose lightly processed foods that have retained most of their original nutritional value:

- whole wheat bread, instead of white
- the whole orange, instead of only the juice
- the whole baked potato, instead of potato chips

You'll consume many more of the harder-to-get vitamins and minerals that are necessary for energy production and muscular contraction.

NEWtrition: Trading In the Old Habits

Is it time to trade in old eating habits for NEWtrition? Today's diet affects this afternoon's training run, tomorrow's race, and your future health. To develop healthier eating patterns takes time but it is a worthwhile investment in yourself.

In January of 1980, a panicked patient came to me. "For my new year's resolutions, I've given up refined sugar, white flour, salt, food additives, and red meat. I've lost six pounds in the past two weeks . . . I'm starving myself! What can I eat?" I interviewed Mark regarding his past and present eating habits, his nutritional goals, and his lifestyle. I concluded that he was changing too much, too fast.

"Your eating habits are a well established part of your lifestyle. To change them all at once is unrealistic and psychologically demanding." I supported his desire to trade in his traditional high salt, high cholesterol, and high protein diet for more healthful foods. However, I encouraged

him to take more gradual steps towards a healthier diet by incorporating one small change each month, such as:

January	Hide the salt shaker.
February	Eat a bran muffin instead of a jelly donut for your morning snack.
March	Drink only one cup of coffee in the morning, and decaffeinated the rest of the day.
April	Bring a jar of old fashioned peanut butter—which is lower in

saturated fat than the regular
type—and a box of stoned wheat
crackers to work, so that you will
have a readily accessible
alternative to the candy
machine.

May   Trade in butter for soft corn oil
or safflower oil margarine, which
comes in a tub.

June   Drink low-fat instead of whole
milk.

When I saw Mark at a race this summer, he felt super
and was pleased with his successful changes. He was
learning to like the foods which contributed to his health. "I
still can't go without my daily ice cream fix", he confessed,
"but I've certainly improved my eating habits in general. I
feel better both physically and psychologically."

Instead of going "cold turkey," I recommend gradually
making small changes and taking deliberate steps toward
the following dietary goals:

1. Eat more chicken, turkey, fish, beans, and nuts
instead of red meats and fatty protein foods such as sausage,
bologna, and bacon. You'll consume less cholesterol and
saturated fats, which are two culprits of heart disease.
Athletes are not immune from heart attacks, they can only
act to prevent them.

2. Eat more cereals and breads at breakfast
instead of bacon and eggs. Again, less cholesterol, less fat.
These carbohydrates are not only a heart-healthy choice, but
also are preferred energy source for your muscles. Athletes
perform best on a high carbohydrate diet.

3. Eat more fruits for snacks and desserts, less
cookies, candy, and other high-calorie-low-nutrient junk
foods. Sugary sweets cause a sugar "high" followed by a

sugar "low," commonly referred to as hypoglycemia. You'll feel shaky, irritable, and unable to perform at your best.

4. Drink more juice and low-fat milk instead of sugary soda and sweetened beverages. You'll replace not only fluid losses but also potassium, calcium, and other electrolytes lost along with water in the sweat.

5. Use less salt, soy sauce, and bouillon when cooking. Remove the salt shaker from the table. Enjoy the natural taste of food along with the peace of mind that you are controlling your blood pressure. You do lose some salt when you sweat, but you do not become depleted. You can

Minerals

Minerals are basic elements found in the soil. These are nutrients picked up by the plants. Humans eat the plants, or the meat from animals that ate the plants, and obtain the needed minerals.

A 150-pound man contains about seven pounds of minerals. He has enought salt to fill a small salt shaker; enough iron for three hairpins; and enough calcium phosphate to sculpt a figurine.

Some minerals are found in only tiny amounts and are called "trace elements." For example, the RDA for iodine is 150 micrograms. One level teaspoon of iodine is 5,000,000 micrograms. You need only a trace amount of iodine to satisfy your body's requirement.

easily replace the loss with salt that is found naturally in the foods you eat.

6. Enjoy beer and wine in moderation. After exercising, alcohol is a poor fluid replacement since it is dehydrating. Alcohol inhibits the secretion of aldosterone, a hormone that retains body water. Without aldosterone you urinate more frequently, hence lose more fluids. Water and juice are best for quenching thirst.

Over the course of the next several months I hope that you will learn to choose food more wisely than you may have in the past. By doing so, you can train your appetite to like those foods that will help you feel healthy and perform at your best. Your muscles, after all, deserve to be fueled with premium nutrition.

The Vital Vitamins: Do active people need more?

Vitamins are metabolic catalysts; they regulate the chemical reactions within the body. They are chemical substances that the body cannot manufacture, thus you must obtain them from the foods you eat. To date, scientists have discovered 13 vitamins, each of which has a specific function. For example:

- Thiamin (B_1) helps convert glucose into energy.
- Vitamin D controls the way your body uses calcium in bones.
- Vitamin A is part of an eye pigment that helps you to see in dim light.

In the appendix I have outlined the functions of some other nutrients.

Although it seems logical that you will need more vitamins to care for your active body, the research studies to date indicate no significantly greater need. The requirement for the B-vitamins is based upon your caloric intake. For

example, the RDA for thiamin (B_1) is 0.5 milligram per 1000 calories. You easily get this amount when you eat larger than normal portions of wholesome food to satisfy your "athlete's appetite." If you should eat poorly and not meet the 2-2-4-4 food plan recommendations, you will not become deficient overnight. All of the vitamins are stored in your body: vitamins B and C in small amounts, A, D, E, and K in stockpiles. You can go for a week or so with no vitamins, with no detrimental effect on your exercise ability. In a study that withheld the B vitamin folic acid, the subjects showed no deficiency symptoms for 20 weeks; with vitamin C, 19 weeks.

Many athletes with whom I talk want to saturate their bodies with vitamins. They believe "If a few are good, a lot will be better." This is NOT true. Vitamins are like spark plugs in a car. A few extras won't make the engine run stronger.

Food supplements will NOT:

- Increase performance
- Increase strength or endurance
- Prevent injuries or illness
- Provide energy
- Build muscles

Most athletes consume a variety of wholesome foods. They receive excessive amounts of vitamins just through their daily diet. For example, one 6-ounce glass of orange juice provides 100% of the recommended daily allowance for

Do Athletes Need Extra Vitamins?

Athletes can get the necessary protein, vitamins, and minerals—except possibly for iron—by eating 1200-1500 calories of wholesome foods according to the 2-2-4-4 food plan. Look at this sample diet which offers the minimal:

> two servings of dairy products
> two servings of protein foods
> four servings of fruits and vegetables
> four servings of breads and cereals

Breakfast:

4-oz. orange juice (made from frozen concentrate)
¾ cup bran flakes with a small banana
8-oz. low-fat milk

Lunch:

1 peanut butter sandwich on whole wheat bread

Snack:

4 rye crackers with Swiss cheese (1½ oz.)

Dinner:

¼ baked chicken
1 boiled potato (medium size)
¾ cup peas and carrots (canned)

This skeletal diet supplies:

1300 calories:	This is half the needs of an active woman.
74 gm. of protein:	The RDA is 56 gm. for a 150-pound man.
860 mg. calcium:	The RDA is 800 mg.
85 mg. vitamin C:	The RDA is 60 mg.
1.2 gm. thiamin:	The RDA is 1 mg./2000 calories; 0.7 mg. for this diet.
8.4 gm. iron:	The RDA is 10 mg. for men; 18 mg. for women.*

Athletes need more calories in addition to this skeletal diet. By adding:

a larger glass of orange juice and an English muffin to breakfast
a glass or milk and four fig bars to lunch
an 8-ounce glass of tomato juice to a snack
a salad with ½ green pepper, a small tomato, and oil and vinegar, and ½ cup ice cream to dinner . . .

you increase:

the calories to 2200:	Sufficient for a lightly exercising woman
the protein to 99 gm:	Almost twice the needs of a 150-pound man
the calcium to 1450 mg:	Almost double the RDA
the thiamin to 1635 mg:	Enough for a person who burns 3000 calories per day
the iron to 15 mg:	150% of the needs of a man, but still slightly under a woman's optimal intake

This 2200-calorie diet is half the food many athletes consume. You get plenty of extra nutrients while satisfying your appetite. The more you eat, the more vitamins, minerals, and protein you give your body.

*The iron requirement is unrealistically high. You actually need only one-tenth of the recommended amount. Since iron is poorly absorbed, the high RDA allows for a large margin of safety. To meet the RDA, men—and especially women—have to carefully select foods for iron content. If you are inclined to be deficient, your body will normally absorb more iron.

vitamin C. Thirsty athletes who guzzle the whole quart get five times what they need. In 1200 to 1500 calories from dairy products, fruits, vegetables, grains, and protein foods, you can satisfy your vitamin requirements. The ravenous athlete easily consumes two to three times that number of calories. Even if some calories are from junk food, you're nutritionally safe. Vitamin supplements are an unnecessary expense. I recommend that you spend your money instead on more fruits and vegetables.

Will meeting the RDA be sufficient? The National Academy of Sciences established the Recommended Daily Allowance as a guideline for determining dietary needs. The RDA is based on requirements of average healthy people.

A large margin of safety is allowed to accommodate the unusual person who has higher metabolic demands, such as with illness. The RDA is not a minimal amount. For example, the body needs ten milligrams of vitamin C to prevent the deficiency disease, scurvy. Thirty milligrams is the minimal daily requirement. Sixty milligrams is the recommended daily allowance.

Will extra vitamins hurt me? Some athletes insist on taking vitamins for peace of mind. They are afraid that their pill-popping competitors will have a winning edge. They also

---

Vitamin A: A Vitamin That Can Be Fatal

Arctic explorers who ate polar bear liver (an unusually high source of vitamin A) became deathly ill from eating a toxic amount of the vitamin. You, too, can eat too much vitamin A. If you take more than 25,000 International Units (I.U.) of vitamin A for several months, you may experience an overdose. The vitamin is stored in your fat and liver and can accumulate to toxic levels. Toxic symptoms include headache, nausea, difficulty sleeping, blurred vision, hair loss, and scaly skin.

The following foods will supply 100% of the recommended daily allowance for vitamin A:

Dark Colored Vegetables

½ medium	carrot
1/3 cup	spinach
2/3 cup	winter squash
3 large	tomatoes

Liver

½ oz.	beef liver
½ medium	chicken liver

RDA = 5000 I.U.

---

like the thought of having "nutritional insurance" in case they eat poorly. I counselled Tom Miller, a tennis player who spent $37 per week on vitamins A, C, D, B-complex, calcium, lecithin, bee pollen, and assorted extracts. He'd have them for breakfast and then dash off to work. "I never have the time to eat meals, so I rely on vitamins. I seem to lack energy though. Do you think I should take vitamin E?"

"Vitamins don't supply energy, Tom. They act in conjunction with some enzymes which convert foods into energy. You still need to eat well."

I taught Tom how to incorporate eating nutritious snacks into his training program. He resolved his energy—as well as his economic—problem. Keep in mind that supplements may have only 8 or 10 of the 13 vitamins and more than 40 nutrients we need from food. You will still need to eat a well-balanced diet regardless of the number of pills you take.

What about megadoses? Megadoses of vitamins (greater than ten times the RDA) may be potentially dangerous. A vitamin is a chemical. Do you avoid chemicals added to your food? I recommend also avoiding abnormally large amounts of chemicals in the vitamin and mineral supplements that you swallow. Most of the B- and C-vitamins will be excreted, but vitamins A, D, E, and K are stored in the fat cells where they may accumulate to toxic levels. The long-term effects of megadoses are not yet evident. They probably won't help you and they may even harm you. Vitamins are chemical substances with specific functions. Excessive amounts of vitamins take on other chemical activity and may become dangerous. The body functions best when its systems are in balance. A large dose of vitamins may upset that balance. [For example, megadoses of vitamin C destroy vitamin B_{12}.] Vitamins from the food you eat are sufficient. You don't need vitamins from pills.

Remember also that many vitamins work in conjunction with others. For example: vitamin C helps iron to be absorbed; vitamin D works with calcium to make strong bones. If you take a pill, you may not be getting the right combination. Nutrition is a new science, with new findings each week. Will megadoses be the next poison associated with cancer—or will they be the next cure for cancer? To date, the answer is unknown. We have a lot to learn.

Ironing Out Your Performance Problems

Do you often wonder if you have iron-poor blood? A Swedish study involving male long distance runners indicated that athletes who train heavily (55-70 miles per week for at least five years) may have a greater tendency toward iron-deficiency anemia. Blood tests on the runners indicated normal iron levels. However, bone marrow tests indicated abnormally low, or non-existent iron stores. They were not anemic but their iron stores were deficient. Anemia occurs when you eat insufficient iron needed to form healthy red blood cells. Iron is an important part of these cells; it helps to transport oxygen from the lungs to the working muscles. With an iron deficiency, your muscles will lack sufficient oxygen. Lactic acid will accumulate and you will fatigue more quickly. You lose trace amounts of iron in sweat. For inactive people these losses are minimal. For heavily training athletes who may lose one to three quarts of sweat per day, the iron losses could add up to one milligram daily.

Iron is important for optimum exercise ability. The recommended daily intake is 10 milligrams for men and 18 for women. (Women require more since they lose iron through menstrual bleeding. Many women athletes stop menstruating. Hence, they do not need extra iron.) Consuming this recommended amount is difficult for the average American.

The following list indicates the iron content of popular foods. To determine if you meet the RDA, add up the milligrams of iron you consume in a day.

Food	Iron (mg.)
liver, 3 oz.	7
turkey	5
pork	5
beef	4
chicken	1
fish	1
egg, 1 large	1
apricots, 12 dried	6
prune juice, ½ cup	5
dates, 9 dried	5
raisins, ½ cup	2
spinach, ½ cup	2
peas, ½ cup	1
baked beans, ½ cup	3
kidney beans, ½ cup	3
bean curd (tofu), 4 oz.	2

Food	Iron (mg.)
*cereal, 100% fortified (MOST, Total) ¾ cup	18
*Cream of Wheat, ½ cup	9
*Raisin Bran, ¾ cup	5
*bread, 1 sl.	1
*spaghetti, ½ cup	1
molasses, 1 tbsp. blackstrap	3
molasses, 1 tbsp. regular	1
brewer's yeast, 1 tbsp.	2
wheat germ, 1 tbsp.	1

*Commercially enriched with iron [1]

These tips may help you to increase your intake:

- An average of 10% of the iron you eat will be absorbed from the intestines. Vitamin C enhances this process so it is best to eat fruits and vegetables rich in vitamin C (cantaloupe, tomatoes, broccoli, potato) along with foods high in iron. For example, orange juice increases the absorption of the iron in enriched breakfast cereals by 250%.

- The tannic acid in tea interferes with the absorption of iron by approximately 50%. Drinking tea with all of your meals is a poor choice. Coffee also reduces iron absorption.

- The iron in meat and animal products is absorbed twice as efficiently as that in vegetables. Popeye may have been strong to the finish—but not because of the iron from the spinach (only 2% of which may be absorbed)!

- Meat enhances the absorption of iron in vegetables. Eat them together for greater nutritional value.

---

[1] Source: J. Pennington and H. Church. *Bowes and Church's Food Values of Portions Commonly Used.* Harper and Row Publishers, N.Y. 1980.

- Iron pots, such as cast-iron skillets, are an excellent source of iron, especially when used for cooking acidic foods. The iron content of spaghetti sauce increases from 3 to 88 milligrams per half cup of sauce when simmered in an iron pot for three hours. Stainless steel cookware may look nice, but it isn't nearly as nutritious as those old skillets your grandmother used.

- Many athletes prefer to limit their intake of red meats such as beef, pork, liver, and ham, which are some of the best sources of iron. Instead they eat iron-poor cheese, yogurt, and dairy products. Eggs provide some iron but it is in a poorly absorbed form.

- If you eat very little red meat you can still get sufficient iron by choosing breads and cereals that have "enriched" or "fortified" written on the label. Compare the nutrition information on the cereal boxes:

  > Quaker 100% Natural™ meets 2% of the RDA for iron. Kellogg's MOST™ meets 100% of the RDA for iron.

So-called "natural foods" and those purchased in health-food stores may not be the wisest choice. "Enriched" whole wheat flour, for example, has more iron than whole wheat flour with "no additives." (See the Bread section for more information).

Carbohydrates: Simple vs. Complex

"The nutrition articles recommend that I eat more complex carbohydrates, and stay away from the simple sugars. I'd be glad to do this—if I only knew what foods these are!" Like many athletes, Jane Pauling is concerned about what she eats, and tries to make wise choices. However, she doesn't always understand what she should do. She asked me to define "simple" and "complex" carbohydrates. Here is the explanation that I gave her:

Simple sugars include glucose, fructose, and galactose (milk sugar). Their chemical formula can be symbolized:

They are monosaccharides (translated: one-sugar). Your body digests all carbohydrates and extra protein into the simple sugar glucose. Simple sugars also include the disaccharides, such as sucrose or table sugar. They are easily digested into glucose. Their chemical formula can be symbolized:

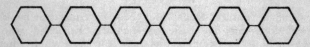

Complex carbohydrates include pasta, bread, cereal, beans, and other starchy foods. These are made from chains of simple sugars:

Plants store extra simple sugars as starch. Have you noticed that sweet peas that are fresh from the garden become starchy as they get older? Humans store extra sugar as glycogen in the muscles and in the liver. Glycogen is your best source of "quick energy."

Both simple and complex carbohydrates are an important part of your diet. You should consume about half of your calories—if not more—from carbohydrates. The trick is to eat more naturally occurring sugars and complex carbohydrates, less refined sugars, such as candy, soda, jelly and refined carbohydrates, such as white flour, cakes, cookies. The difference is that most complex carbohydrates are important natural sources of many essential vitamins, minerals, fiber, and protein. If they are refined, they lose considerable amounts of the valuable nutrients. They will provide energy but little else. They are "empty" calories.

I recommend that you get most of your carbohydrates from the following foods:

> fruits, juice
> vegetables
> dried beans, such as limas, chili beans
> legumes, such as split peas, peanuts
> enriched:
>> hot and cold cereal
>> whole wheat flour
>> whole wheat bread, crackers
>> pasta, noodles
>> barley, oats
>> corn, rice, brown rice

Eat fewer simple sugars and refined carbohydrates:

> sugar, white or brown
> honey
> maple syrup
> white flour, not enriched
> white rice, not enriched

Health-Food Hokum

Will health foods, such as bee pollen, brewer's yeast, and "all-natural" vitamins make you healthier? I doubt it...but there is always that glimmer of hope. Most people, especially athletes, are believers. That is, we act out of belief rather than knowledge. When health-food promoters peddle their promises—"Doc Snozum's Secret Formula will solve your problems"—the hopeful believers buy them in their search for a fountain of youth, a cure-all, a super-pill, or even a love potion.

Health-promisers make their fortunes by exploiting this tendency, which is only human. We can't know everything. We can't always tell fact from fiction. We can, however, learn

how to arrive at our beliefs. We should value knowledge rather than blind promises. Before you swallow the health-food hokum, assess the claims. Are they based on scientific information? By definition, scientific information:

- Defines any given situation. For example, "Do you sleep poorly?" vs. the more precisely qualifying "Do you sleep poorly after drinking coffee with dinner?"

- Explains logically how things work: "Extra vitamins will give you renewed energy" vs. the explanatory, "B-vitamins are important for converting the foods we eat into energy."

- Compares an experimental group with a control group: "After taking this super-pill, I felt so much stronger." vs. "The twenty subjects who took the super-pill exercised twenty-five minutes longer than the control group who were given a placebo."

As humans, we will never be authorities on everything. But we don't have to be ignorant either. Before spending your money on metabolic magic, I recommend that you carefully assess the situation. Are you making your decision based on scientific information or on the hope of purchasing a cure-all, catch-all answer?

For additional reading on health foods I recommend *The Health Robbers* by S. Barrett and G. Knight, Stickley Co., Philadelphia, 1976, and *The New Nuts Among the Berries* by R. Deutsch, Bull Publishing, Palo Alto, California, 1977.

Shaking the Salt Habit

Do you salt your food before you taste it? Munch on pretzels, salted peanuts, and popcorn? Finish off the crumbs in the bottom of the cracker box? Well—now is the time for you to shake the salt habit!

Salt is a combination of two minerals: sodium and chloride. Although some sodium is important for maintaining proper fluid balance between the water in and around your cells and in your blood, too much sodium lays the foundation for high blood pressure, heart attacks, stroke, and kidney failure. An average American easily eats 10 to 60 times the 0.2 grams of sodium needed to replace daily losses. Even if you choose foods that are not salty and add no table salt, you may still consume 2 to 3 grams of sodium. Meats, fish, dairy products, vegetables, and grains naturally contain sodium. How much is a gram of sodium? One level teaspoon of salt (40% sodium) contains about 2.3 grams, or 2300 milligrams of sodium. An adequate and safe sodium intake is between 1.1 and 3.3 grams.

On the daily basis, I recommend that you take steps toward shaking the salt habit:

- Remove the salt shaker from the table. Train your taste buds to appreciate the flavor of the food rather than the flavor of the salt.

- Use half the amount of salt when cooking and baking (except in yeast breads). For flavor, add any of the following:

pepper	wine	onion	vanilla
herbs	sherry	garlic	flavorings
spices	vinegar	horseradish	lemon

Foods Low in Sodium

	mg. sodium		mg. sodium
1 oz. chicken, plain	20	½ cup fresh fruit	5
2 tbsp. peanut butter	50	½ cup fresh vegetables	10
1 medium egg	60	1 cup pasta, unsalted	5
½ cup ice cream	50	1 sl. bread	150
8 oz. milk	125	1 oz. dry cereal	250
8 oz. yogurt	125	1 pat margarine	50
Adequate intake	2000 mg.		

Source: J. Pennington and H. Church. *Bowes and Church's Food Values of Portions Commonly Used.* Harper and Row Publishers, N.Y. 1980.

- Try to avoid convenience foods such as TV dinners, packaged meals, canned soups, instant oatmeal. In addition to salt, these contain sodium additives:

  monosodium glutamate (MSG)   sodium proprionate
  disodium phosphate   sodium benzoate

- Buy foods in their natural state:

freshly shelled peanuts	10 mg. / cup
canned, salted peanuts	600 mg. / cup
fresh green beans	5 mg. / cup
canned green beans	320 / cup

- Limit your intake of:

soy sauce	catsup	Worcestershire	pickles
MSG	mustard	steak sauce	olives

- Sodium in sea salt is just as potentially hazardous as sodium in table salt.

For you to acquire the taste for salt-free food may take time but the effort is an excellent investment in your future health.

Do athletes need extra salt in hot weather? Athletes who sweat do lose some sodium but do *not* become depleted. Sweat has proportionally less sodium when compared to your blood and intracellular fluid. Replacing the sodium is secondary to replacing the water. Here is why:

	mg. sodium
One liter sweat	0.9-1.4
Average 150 lb. body	90
Adequate dietary intake (if no heavy sweating)	2
Average American diet	4-12

Foods High in Sodium

	mg. sodium
Processed meats:	
1 oz. raw bacon	110
1 oz. canned ham	280
1 oz. bologna	360
1-2 oz. hotdog	550
Cheese:	
1 oz. cheddar	220
½ cup cottage	250
1 oz. American	320
Processed foods:	
½ cup vegetables, canned	200
½ cup tomato juice	250
1 cube bouillon	960
1 turkey pot pie	1100
1 chicken TV dinner	1100
1 cup spaghetti, canned	1220
½ can vegetable soup	1250
Condiments:	
1 tsp. mustard	65
1 tbsp. catsup	155
1 tbsp. French dressing	200
1 packet (¼ tsp.) salt	500
1 tbsp. soy sauce	860
Snacks:	
¼ cup peanuts (salted)	150
10 potato chips	200
2 Hostess Twinkies	400
2 lg. pickle spears	700

Source: J. Pennington and H. Church. *Bowes and Church's Food Values of Portions Commonly Used.* Harper and Row, Publishers, N.Y. 1980.

Athletes who train in the heat sweat less sodium (but more water) than an inactive person. The long distance runner who trains for 20 miles in a 60°F. summer's day may lose 1.85 to 5.50 grams of sodium. To replace this sodium during exercise is unnecessary. The amount of sodium in your blood actually increases with heavy sweating. You lose proportionately more water than sodium. Your need to replace body water is greater than any immediate demands for electrolytes. Keep this in mind: if you do need salt, you will crave it.

Salt tablets are unnecessary—and may even be potentially dangerous. They dehydrate your body by drawing water from the body tissues into your stomach to dilute the high sodium concentration from the tablet. Replacing sodium losses is easy. Most foods other than fresh fruits and vegetables contain significant amounts of sodium.

Chapter 3
Smart Shopping

Good eating habits start in the super market! I suggest you become a smart shopper and help yourself to good health. Learn these tips:

- Make a list—you'll remember everything you need and won't end up with a lot of extra goodies.

- Shop when you are well fed. This will help you to steer clear of the sweets, candy, soda, chips, and other junk food that provides expensive calories with few vitamins or minerals.

- Read labels to check for recommended oils (safflower,

corn, sunflower) rather than hydrogenated vegetable oil, coconut oil, palm oil, or lard.

- Don't be fooled by the label.

  "Low-fat" or "fat-free" doesn't always mean low calorie. Fruit flavored yogurt may be low in fat but high in sugar calories. Fat-free Syrian bread is similar to most other sandwich breads in that fat is usually a minor ingredient.

  "Sugar-free" foods may still have sugar, but in a disguised form, such as honey, corn syrup, xylitol, or sorbitol. (These other sugars break down to glucose in the body.) Sugar-free gum, for example, has 7 calories of sorbitol in each stick.

  Products that "contain no cholesterol" may be loaded with the even more undesirable saturated fats. Peanut butter has no cholesterol but processed peanut butter has saturated fat. The process of hydrogenation converts liquid unsaturated fats into a solid saturated fat, creating a food that is no longer heart-healthy. See the section "What about cholesterol?" for more information.

  "Imitation" products can be a better choice than the real thing. With imitation dairy products, for example, the cream content is lower than

---

Hidden Sugars When you read food labels, watch out for the following "hidden sugars" listed among the ingredients:

corn syrup	glucose	maltose
dextrose	honey	maple syrup
fructose	invert sugar	molasses
galactose	lactose	sucrose

What Is A Calorie?

When food is metabolized in the body it releases energy and heat that can be measured in calories. One calorie is the amount of heat required to raise the temperature of one liter of water one degree centigrade.

All foods supply calories:

Carbohydrates	4 calories per gm.
Protein	4
Alcohol	7
Fat	9

Vitamins, minerals, and water do not provide calories. They are, however, essential for making your body function properly.

The amount of carbohydrate, protein, and fat in a food determines the caloric value of the food. By using information on food labels you can calculate the source of your calories. For example, by reading the label on the milk carton, I know that milk has:

8 grams of fat
8 grams of protein
11 grams of carbohydrate

I multiply the number of grams by the calories per gram:

11 gm. Carbohydrate	8 gm. Protein	8 gm. Fat
x 4 calories	x 4	x 9
44 calories	32	72

Total calories = 148 per 8 ounces

I have learned that 72 of the 148 calories in a glass of whole milk come from the fat content. That is a lot! That is why I prefer to drink low-fat milk, which provides 18 of the 110 calories from fat.

government regulations. Imitation cream cheese
has less fat and half the calories of the standard
product.

* Be aware that ingredients are listed separately by weight
from most to least. The granola with rolled oats, wheat
germ, sunflower seeds, and raisins will have more nutritional value than that with brown sugar, honey, and oil at
the top of the list.

I recommend that athletes read food labels for undesirable
fat content when selecting food for carbohydrate-loading.
Your small scoop of ice cream with 10 grams of fat will provide

90 of the 170 calories from fat. (1 gram fat= 9 calories.) You won't store the fat calories as glycogen. By reading the sherbert or ice milk label, you will discover that these desserts are a higher carbohydrate, lower fat choice. I always teach weight watchers to read the label for calorie content and to pay attention to portion size. Are you eating one ounce of Syrian bread for 55 calories—or the whole five-ounce loaf for 275 calories?

Your Supply Cupboard

I always stock basic foods that won't spoil quickly. On those days when I come home to an empty refrigerator, I can at least create a tasty meal from the stand-bys. Or, when greeted by unexpected company I don't panic. I can easily serve an impromptu but impressive meal . . . my choice of:

Sesame Chicken with stuffing and broccoli
Spaghetti á la Carbonara with carrot sticks
Mushroom Pizza
Tuna Noodle Casserole with peas
French Cheese Sandwiches with three bean salad
Corn Chowder with hot biscuits and celery sticks

My Standard Ingredients

Cupboard:
  noodles
  spaghetti
  rice
  biscuit mix
  flour
  baking soda
  baking powder
  bouillon cubes
  corn oil
  chili sauce
  sherry

white wine
molasses
onions

Refrigerator:
  eggs
  cheese
  parmesan cheese
  margarine
  celery
  carrots
  yeast

Cans of:
  tomato puree
  crushed tomatoes
  mushrooms
  green beans
  yellow beans
  kidney beans
  cream of mushroom soup
  dried onion soup
  evaporated milk
  powdered milk
  tuna

Spice rack:
  salt
  pepper
  cinnamon
  soy sauce
  basil
  curry
  garlic powder
  oregano
  Italian salad dressing mix
  sesame seeds

Freezer:
  wheat bread
  Syrian bread
  broccoli
  peas
  corn
  chicken pieces (wrapped
    individually)

Words of Wisdom

Cooking can be fun. And it can also be frustrating. In order to get the most enjoyment from meal preparations, consider these words of wisdom that I offer you:

- Read the recipe through before you start start cooking. Become familiar with the procedures and the time commitment.

- Check to see if you have all the ingredients— or substitutions—on hand.

Words of Wisdom

Feel free to make changes, add vegetables, subtract spices, top with cheese, or make many other simple variations.

- Before serving a new recipe to company, first cook it for yourself. This may save you an embarrassing memory.

- When entertaining, either:

  Put your guests to work. Solicit their help with chopping, stirring, etc. Sharing the meal preparation can be as friendly as sharing the meal. Or:

  Prepare the meal ahead of time, so that you can relax with your guests. Pre-make a casserole or hearty soup. Serve with a salad and fresh bread.

By carefully planning the menu, you can enjoy both the dinner and the company of your friends.

- Cook too much, rather than too little. Enjoy the leftovers either for lunch or dinner the next day. What a pleasure to come home to a ready-made meal! Warm it in the oven while you go out for a jog after work.

Chapter 4
Breakfast

The typical American breakfast is NO breakfast. Many breakfast-skippers say they aren't hungry. But perhaps a whole bag of cookies was eaten last night in place of an early breakfast. I recommend that a well-intentioned weight-watcher not try to save 300 calories by omitting the morning meal. At the end of a hard day, when you're tired and hungry, you can too easily rationalize why you deserve the ice cream sundae! Late night snacks frequently contain twice the calories of the cereal and juice but half the vitamins and minerals. The majority of the overweight patients I counsel are breakfast-skippers. "No time," "I'm not hungry," "I don't like cereal or eggs," are the most common excuses.

Sugar Content of Some Breakfast Cereals

Cereal	% Sugar
Shredded Wheat (large biscuit)	1.0
Cheerios	2.2
Puffed Rice	2.4
Wheat Chex	2.6
Product 19	4.1
Special K	4.4
Wheaties	4.7
Grape-nuts	6.6
Corn Flakes (Kellogg)	7.7
Rice Krispies	10.0
Raisin Bran (Kellogg)	10.6
Life	14.5
40% Bran Flakes (Post)	15.0
100% Bran	18.9
100% Natural with brown sugar and honey	22.0
Heartland	23.0
Country Morning	31.0
Sugar Pops	37.0
Cap'n Crunch	43.0
Frosted Flakes	44.0
Froot Loops	47.4
Apple Jacks	55.0
Sugar Smacks	61.3

Source: *Journal of Dentistry for Children*, Sept.-Oct. 1974.

One patient refused to eat breakfast because, "Once I start to eat, I can't stop all day." Mary ate only at night—but what a meal! A fattening 2500-calorie feast. She ate ravenously to satisfy the hunger that she'd squelched all day. After the dinner she'd nibble 500 more calories from popcorn, peanuts, crackers, and cheese. "I don't eat any of the fattening junk," Mary declared. Although Mary chose only wholesome foods, she chose too many calories. I convinced her to try, for one week, to eat three meals on a regular schedule. She lost ten pounds in a month. At her last visit she commented, "I now prefer to go to bed a little hungry. I sleep better, and I look forward to eating a nice breakfast in the morning. I feel perkier at work, too."

Breakfast IS an important meal of the day. Eating food for fuel when you need it during the daytime is more sensible than sleeping on it at night. Breakfast-eaters feel better physically and mentally. You are alert and productive in the morning. The abstainers more readily succumb to the mid-morning droop. You may buy "waist-ful" donuts and pastries for needed energy.

Hikers and bicyclists who plan an all day excursion will benefit from a substantial breakfast. You should choose carbohydrate foods—hot cereal, french toast—since they will easily digest while you exercise. A hearty ham and eggs breakfast will sit in your stomach and be carried along for the ride. Small amounts of protein—such as one egg, a slice of cheese, a tablespoon of peanutbutter—are okay. They do take longer to leave the stomach—but they "stick to your ribs"—and keep you feeling satisfied for longer without being a burden.

I recommend that runners who train at lunch hour eat a low-fat breakfast. By noon, this meal will be digested and ready to provide energy. You won't be "starving to death" and will better enjoy your run.

My low-fat breakfast suggestions include:

Hot cereal with raisins
Cold cereal with skim milk
Whole wheat toast with jam
English muffins
Biscuits with honey
Plain muffins (corn, bran, apple)
Banana and other fruits
Syrian bread, toasted with low-fat cheese

Refer to the section on "Pre-competition Meals" for more information about eating before exercising.

For me breakfast has to be quick and easy. I prefer to sleep an additional 20 minutes rather than putter around the kitchen. Here are some of my suggestions.

Cereal: Some like it cold

Some cold cereals have added sugar. They are, nevertheless, good sources of B-vitamins and iron if you can find the words "fortified" or "enriched" printed on the label. Some cereal labels list the grams of sugar per serving. Four grams of sugar equal one teaspoon. One teaspoon of sugar has sixteen calories.

1 oz.	Cereal	gms.	tsps.	Sugar Calories
¼ cup	100% Natural™ (Quaker)	9	2¼	36
2/3 cup	40% Bran Flakes (Kellogg)	6	1½	24
¾ cup	Honey Nut Cheerios™ (General Mills)	10	2 1/3	40

Adding sugar to cold cereal does not ruin its nutritional value. The cereal still provides vitamins and minerals along with the sugar, in the same way that orange juice provides nutrients along with its natural sugar. (All of the calories in orange juice are from sugar.) Your body does not differentiate between "natural" and "refined" sugars.

- So called "natural cereals" with *no additives* generally have no vitamins or iron added. Wiser choices are "enriched" whole grain cereals such as Raisin Bran, Oat Flakes, and Wheat Chex.™

- High fiber bran cereals are the best choice for preventing constipation. Fiber is the part of plants that cannot be digested by man. It absorbs water, which makes the stool softer and easier to eliminate. Bran is the most concentrated source of fiber. I recommend eating bran cereals. This is an easy way to increase your fiber intake to the recommended five to six grams per day.

Cereal		Fiber/(1 oz. Serving)
Raw milled bran		3.3
Wheat Bran	All Bran, Bran Buds, 100% Bran	2.1
Mixed	Familia	1.2
Wheat Bran	40% Bran Flakes, Raisin Bran	.0
Wheat	Puffed Wheat, Shredded Wheat, Total, Wheaties	.7
Cooked	Farina, Oatmeal, Wheatena, Ralston	.6
Wheat, Barley	Grape-nuts, Grape-nut Flakes	.5
Oats	Fortified Oat Flakes, Cheerios, Life	.3
Rice	Puffed Rice, Rice Krispies	.3
Mixed	Special K, Product 19, Quaker 100% Natural	.1
Corn	Corn Flakes	.1

- You can save money by adding your own raisins to 40% Bran Flakes. They will be moister and easier to chew.

---

[1] Source: *The Medical Letter,* Nov. 7, 1975.
56 Harrison St., New Rochelle, N.Y.

- If you combine two or three cereals, you will discover new tastes and get greater nutritional value. I like mixing Grape-nuts™ with Wheat Chex.™

- If you are watching your weight dilute (mix) high-calorie granola with lower-calorie flake cereals. I sprinkle granola on top of 40% Bran Flakes.™

- Try flavoring your cereal milk with vanilla or molasses. Use yogurt instead of milk.

Cereal: Some like it hot

Hot cereal can be a very gentle way to start your day. I recommend that you try:

- Cooking hot cereal with milk in place of water for more nutritional value.

- Combine two or three hot cereals for a taste change. Mix wheatena and oatmeal. Even granola can be cooked. I sometimes add cooked rice.

- Hot cereal will "stick to your ribs" if you add a source of fat. When I'm camping I always add margarine, peanut butter, or walnuts. Otherwise the cereal "disappears" in about 1½ hours, leaving me hungry. Fat takes longer to digest than the carbohydrates in the cereal.

- Add fresh or dried fruits: apple, banana, pineapple, raisins, dates, apricots.

- Top with applesauce, cinnamon, canned fruit, granola, sesame seeds, walnuts, yogurt, cottage cheese.

Non-Breakfasts

Breakfast can be more imaginative than toast or eggs. Try:

- Fruit pizza: Spread Syrian bread with cottage or ricotta cheese, top with sliced fruit; broil.

- English muffin pizza: Put pizza sauce and cheese on muffin halves; broil.

- Easy cheese Danish: Spread toast with cottage cheese or low-fat cream cheese, sprinkle with cinnamon; broil. Poppy seeds or sesame seeds add a creative crunch!

- Nothing is wrong with a tuna, grilled cheese, or peanut butter sandwich.

- Soup: Why not? It'll warm you up, and stick with you.

- Leftovers: Enjoy last night's memories for this morning's energy boost. Tuna noodle casserole, pizza, chicken or whatever.

Eat-on-the-run Breakfasts

Does your morning training interfere with breakfast? If you exercise when you first get up in the morning you may not be hungry by the time you have to leave for work. If you know that you won't have, make, or take the time in the morning, pack breakfast the night before and grab it as you run out the door. Enjoy it as you wait for the bus or walk to work. Some examples of breakfasts to grab include:

Chunk of cheese
Yogurt
Banana
Raisins and peanuts
Bran muffin with peanut butter
Bagel with low-fat cream cheese
Syrian bread with sliced cheese
Peanut butter crackers

In 1977, I worked in Worcester, Massachusetts and I commuted one hour each morning. No matter what time I got out of bed I always ate a rushed breakfast. One day I took my breakfast with me in the car. What a great idea! I enjoyed a leisurely meal while listening to music. The commute became much more pleasurable, and my stomach appreciated the relaxed meal.

Blender Breakfasts

Blender breakfasts are a quick and easy way to combine foods. Be creative! Two suggestions are:

Milk and/or yogurt with strawberries
Orange Juice and a banana and dried milk

I have included some other suggestions in the section on Fluids.

Does Coffee Keep You Perking?

Many of my patients admit, with guilt, that they drink coffee. They consider it an addicting "poison." Research studies indicate that your morning cup of coffee is okay—enjoy it guilt-free. However, I do not recommend too much caffeine (more than two or three cups) throughout the day since it may lead to nervousness and restless sleep.

As you sip your coffee, ponder these bits of information:

- More than 250 milligrams of caffeine per day is considered excessive. Drip coffee, such as you get in a restaurant, has 145 milligrams of caffeine per small (5-ounce) cup. Instant coffee has less than half that number—65 milligrams. Remember that a large mug holds twice that amount of coffee—and caffeine.

- Tea brewed for five minutes has 45 milligrams per cup. The quick, one-minute brew has 30.

- Colas, such as Coke™, Tab™, and Pepsi™, have about 50 milligrams of caffeine per can. A can of Coke™ for a small child is the equivalent of two cups of coffee for an adult. Root beer is a caffeine-free alternative.

- Coffee is not directly associated with heart disease. Coffee combined with cigarettes, however, results in in higher incidence of cardiovascular problems.

- Drinking coffee or tea with meals interferes with the absorption of thiamin by 75% and iron by 90%.

- To reduce your caffeine intake, try:

  decaffeinated coffee-- contains a small amount of caffeine (1 mg./8 oz.)
  Postum,™, Pero™ -- coffee substitutes
  hot water with lemon-- warmer than Perrier™ with lime
  herbal tea -- Sleepytime™ and chamomile are pleasant choices
  broth, bouillon -- homemade will have less salt

Caffeine Content of Common Beverages

	mg./5 oz. cup
Coffee:	
drip	150
percolated	110
instant	65
decaffeinated	5
Tea:	
5-min. brew	45
1-min. brew	30
Cocoa	15

	mg./12 oz. can
Coke	65
Pepsi	45

Source: Bunker, M. L. and McWilliams, M., "Caffeine Content of Common Beverages" *J. Am. Dietetic Assoc.* 74:28, 1979.

Alba™, Ovaltine™	-- nutritious milk-based drinks
mulled cider	-- heat with cinnamon
hot cranberry juice	-- heat with cloves
taffy milk	-- heat milk with molasses

- Exercise is an excellent healthful stimulant. A quick walk around the block—or even through the building, up and down the stairs—may be what you really need, more than a coffee break.

- For marathon runners and endurance athletes, caffeine may improve exercise capacity. See the section on "Hungry for success" for more information.

Chapter 5

Munch-a-Lunch

"Brown bagging it" may be your last choice for the perfect business lunch, but the advantages are obvious. Packed lunches:

- Save you time, money, and perhaps calories
- Meet your standards of nutrition
- Are readily available in case you get stranded in the office
- Allow you to train during your noon break and then munch your lunch later on.

Most working people and students are too rushed in the morning to make lunch. I recommend the following suggestions for simplicity and variety:

- Make your lunch the night before. Store it in the refrigerator. The thoroughly-chilled food will stay fresher longer.

- Convert dinner leftovers into tomorrow's lunch. Baked chicken makes a fine lunch treat. Even vegetables and casseroles don't have to be eaten hot. They can easily be packed in plastic containers to provide variety.

- Make several sandwiches at one time; store them in the freezer. The frozen sandwich will be thawed—and fresh— by lunchtime. Sliced meats, cheese, margarine, and mustard freeze nicely. Don't freeze eggs, mayonnaise, jelly, lettuce, tomatoes or raw veggies. You'll end up with a very soggy sandwich.

- Store small cans of juice in the freezer. Add one to your lunch bag in the morning. It will keep the other foods chilled and be ready for your enjoyment by noon. (The can will "sweat" so wrap it in a plastic bag.)

- Pack crisp lettuce leaves separately, along with tomatoes for freshness. Add them to your sandwich when you're ready to eat.

- Tired of the same ol' sandwich? Add variety with different breads:

cracked wheat	bagel	pocket bread
honey bran	English muffin	raisin
rye	bulkie roll	brown bread
pumpernickel	onion foll	banana bread

- Does stale bread dry up your appetite? Keep a few fresh loaves in your freezer; remove the slices as you need them. Make the sandwich with frozen bread; it will thaw within minutes.

- Experiment with variations on a theme. Try:

  Peanut butter with: sliced banana, raisins, dates, shredded coconut, sunflower seeds, sesame seeds, apple wedges, celery. Spread it on: bran muffin, date-nut bread, crackers.

Sliced cheese with: oregano, Italian seasoning, green peppers, tomatoes.

Grated cheese with: cottage cheese, Italian seasoning, baked beans, chili beans.

Low-fat cream cheese with: bean sprouts, raisins, dates, cucumber, sliced tomatoes, onions, chives, olives, chopped chutney and curry, sesame, or sunflower seeds.

- Beans: mash some with the back of a fork; add whole beans to this paste so that they stick together. Add catsup to baked beans; sliced tomato and cheese to chili beans.

- Other creative additions include: herbs, such as oregano, garlic, basil, curry powder, sauerkraut, spinach leaves instead of lettuce, salad vegetables.

- Would you enjoy a change from a sandwich? Pack the filling separately. Instead of bread, have whole wheat crackers, bran muffin, melba toast, or bread sticks.

- Do you enjoy a hot lunch? Fill a wide mouth thermos with vegetable soup, chili, or fish chowder.

- In warm weather, enjoy a cold lunch: pack yogurt, fresh fruit cup, three bean salad. Your lunch companions will envy your ingenuity as they eat their sandwiches.

- Are you watching your calories? Then "hold the mayo!" Remember that bread is NOT the calorie culprit. The mayonnaise in the tuna fish, butter in the grilled cheese sandwich, and fatty bacon in the "BLT" are the caloric part of the sandwich. Cut out the fats to cut down the calories.

Grilled cheese sandwich:

2 sl. bread	160 calories
1 sl. cheese	110
butter for grilling	150

Bacon, lettuce and tomato sandwich:

2 sl. bread	160 calories
lettuce, tomato	25
2 tbsp. mayonnaise	200
4 sl. bacon	200

Tuna salad sandwich:

2 sl. bread	160 calories
2 oz. tuna	80
3 tbsp. mayonnaise	300

Calorie conscious deli-delights include: chicken, turkey, lean roast beef, boiled ham, and sliced cheese.

- Do you want a low-calorie spread for a "moistener?" Mustard, catsup, even yogurt, will do the job. For a tasty sandwich I enjoy yogurt, cheese, and sprouts. Mix tuna with yogurt or diet salad dressing (which still has calories, but not as many). You can stretch the filling with low-calorie finely-chopped green pepper, celery, onion, tomato and season it with curry, basil, or Italian seasonings. I enjoy creating new taste treats instead of eating routine foods.

- What's for dessert? Pack fresh fruit, individual canned fruit, yogurt, raisins, dates, apricots, oatmeal cookies, fig bars, granola bars, peanuts, or graham crackers.

- What's to drink? Vary your beverages: low-fat milk, vegetable juice, tomato juice, fruit juice, herbal tea, instant soup, hot cocoa, and bouillon.

Restaurants: Fast and Friendly

When life is keeping you on the run fast-food restaurants may seem the friendly alternative to your empty refrigerator or the bottom of the peanut butter jar. Many of my patients resort to fast-foods, as the alternative to no food. I teach them to choose wisely. Nutritionally the meals can be adequate. A cheeseburger with lettuce and tomato and a can of juice or a cheese pizza with green peppers, mushrooms, and onions are two examples of balanced meals that include a variety of foods from the different food groups. I do not recommend fried fish, french fries, shake, and apple pie—they are loaded with fat, sugar, and many nutritionally empty calories. Within five minutes you can easily chow down half of your daily caloric allottment. The 1000 calories

from the burger, fries, and shake may be burned off by the long distance runner who trains for two hours each day, but if you are a two-mile jogger, beware! You'll have to increase your mileage to ten the next day to use up the calories.

Fast-foods typically lack fiber, vitamins A and C, and are high in fat and salt. When you do eat fast-foods, plan to balance your day's eating. Choose fresh fruits, salad, and vegetables for other meals or snacks; bring along an apple from home for lunch dessert instead of the apple pie; drink a can of juice instead of a soda for your midafternoon snack. Here is a calorie count for some fast-food favorites:

		Calories
McDonald's		
Hamburger		260
Quarter Pounder		420
French fries		210
Shake, chocolate		365
Filet O'Fish		400
Pizza Hut (cheese pizza)		
Whole 10-inch Pizza	— thick crust	1021
	— thin crust	900
1/2 of 13-inch	— thick crust	900
	— thin crust	850
1/2 of 15-inch	— thick crust	1200
	— thin crust	1150
Burger King		
French fries		220
Shake, chocolate		365
Whopper		605
Whaler		485
Kentucky Fried Chicken		
Original Recipe Dinner (3 pieces fried chicken, gravy, mashed potatoes, cole slaw, roll)		830

	Calories
Arthur Treacher's (fish, chips, cole slaw)	
3 piece dinner	1100
2 piece dinner	905
Burger Chef	
Big Chef	540
French fries	190
Shake, chocolate	320
Skipper's Treat	605

Rules for Restaurants

Is dining out a dietary disaster? From experience, I've found the most popular restaurants are those that serve the largest portions. You leave stuffed—you certainly ate your money's worth! But did you also let that huge meal go to waist, rather than to waste? Some athletes burn off the high-calorie restaurant selections: garlic bread saturated with butter, salad smothered with blue cheese dressing, baked potato piled high with sour cream. Many athletes, however, are wise eaters and weight-watchers; they do not compromise on their commitment to healthful eating.

When dining out, these suggestions may help you to control what and how much you eat:

- Patronize restaurants that offer broiled foods, a salad bar, or a variety of sandwiches.

- Specifically ask for cooked foods to be broiled, baked, or boiled and served without added fats. (Many chefs add butter while broiling.) I recommend chicken, turkey, fish, and seafood. They are more healthful choices than red meat and casseroles with rich gravies or sauces.

- Pick broth-based soups such as ministrone or chicken-vegetable. Beware of chowders and cream soups, which are swimming with saturated fats and calories.

- Request that salad dressing be served on the side. I sometimes dilute the salad dressing with vinegar or water. I then enjoy a moist salad without the extra calories.

- Select vegetables without sauces. Request no added butter.

- Enjoy the roll (100 nutritious calories), but skip the butter (100 empty calories).

- Ask for fresh fruit cup, melon, or strawberries for dessert.

- If you want a glass of wine, have that instead of an appetizer, roll, or dessert.

When you are faced with a meal that's a caloric catastrophe, remember that you don't HAVE to eat it all. You can halve it and save it for tomorrow's lunch.

Chapter 6

Energy Lacking?
Try Snacking!

"I never seem to have the time to eat meals. I rush around and grab something to eat when I reach the point of starvation. Snacks are my dietary mainstay." This comment by ballet dancer Sally Thomas sounds familiar to many of us who rely on snacks for energy. I remind my patients that snacking CAN be good for you, assuming that you make wise choices. The number of times that you eat is not as important as what you eat in the course of an entire day. I generally feel droopy at four in the afternoon, so I enjoy a "cracker snack." It perks me up, appeases my hunger, and gives me energy toward my after-work training.

I recommend that you plan a snack as a regular part of

your day. Allow yourself to eat a little something to maintain your energy. Eating four or five smaller meals is less demanding on your system than the "starve and stuff" routine. This mini-meal can offer you an enjoyable and nutritious energy boost. The following suggestions will help those who have trouble breaking the candy and cookie habit. File under "emergency food" a few nutritious snack items:

dry roasted peanuts	dried apples	bread sticks
sunflower seeds	sesame crackers	cans of juice
	peanut butter	raisins

Tending the Vending Machine?

If your only option for a snack is from the vending machine, I suggest that you choose the foods with vitamins, minerals, and protein:

peanuts	milk	granola bar
dried fruit	cheese and crackers	fig bars
juice	peanut butter crackers	

Hankering for chocolate? At least select the candy bar with some nutritional value, such as a peanut butter cup or chocolate with almonds. If the office vending machine offers nothing but junk, I recommend that you check the sides of the machine to find the name of the supply company and give them a call. Suggest a few items that you and your co-workers would enjoy. Having nutritious selections will at least allow you the opportunity to make wise choices.

Pack-a-Snack

When packing your lunch for work add a little something extra for a snack:

apple	banana	carrots	celery sticks
raisins	dates	nuts	sunflower seeds
bagel	cheese	crackers	yogurt

When at home, enjoy creative snacks:

- Make an open-face sandwich.
- Melt cheese on half an english muffin.
- Heat up some vegetable soup.
- Mix yogurt with cinnamon and applesauce.
- Nibble on leftovers.
- Spread apple slices or banana with peanut butter.
- Make "cheesecake"—spread graham crackers with low-fat cream cheese, and strawberry jam.

Searching for Quick Energy?

If you want quick energy, don't run to the candy machine! Quick energy is stored in your muscles as glycogen and is readily available for immediate action. If you eat sugary foods for an energy boost 30–45 minutes before exercising, you may actually hinder your performance by contributing toward hypoglycemia—low blood sugar. The sugar will trigger your pancreas to secrete extra insulin. When combined with exercise, this insulin may cause your blood sugar to drop to an abnormally low level. You may feel light-headed, shaky, uncoordinated, and hungry. For example, hypoglycemia frequently occurs with wrestlers who crash diet before the pre-competition weigh-in. They then proceed to eat candy bars and drink soda as a last minute effort to regain their energy. They become hypoglycemic and perform poorly. To prevent this, I recommend that wrestlers eat low fat foods such as crackers, chicken noodle soup, yogurt, and fruit, rather than sugary sweets.

You don't have to eat sugar, per se for energy. Although simple sugars from fruit, juice, and candy appear most quickly in your blood—5-7 minutes after ingestion—all carbohydrate foods and extra proteins eventually digest into glucose (the simplest sugar). Many carbohydrate foods, such as fruits, juices, and vegetables have a lot of natural sugar as well as vitamins and minerals. If in a day you consume three glasses of orange juice, an apple, and a banana you take in

Exercise physiologist David Costill studied the effect on athletic performance of 300 calories of sugar taken 45 minutes before hard running. The sugar contributed to elevated blood sugar and insulin levels. When the subjects began to exercise hard, the combination of the high insulin and the muscular activity caused the blood sugar to be removed too quickly and it dropped abnormally low. The subjects felt tired, and found the running difficult.

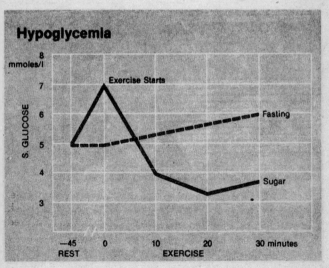

Costill, D. et. al. "Effect of Elevated Plasma FFA and Insulin on Muscle Glycogen Usage During Exercise." *J. Appl. Physio.* 43(4)695,1977.

not only 500 calories of sugar, but also five times the RDA for vitamin C, superfluous amounts of potassium, and some fiber.

For hikers, cyclists, and skiers who are active all day, sweets are acceptable snacks. You will not experience hypoglycemia because exercise reduces insulin secretion. The sugar will enter into your bloodstream and actually prevent you from feeling tired, a key symptom of hypoglycemia. I recommend that you frequently snack

throughout the day on raisins, dates, other fruits and juice. You will feel perkier and maintain your stamina.

I sometimes have a low-energy day when I crave for something super-sweet, gooey, non-nutritious. I know that to occasionally succumb to this urge is okay. I relax, savor the flavor, and enjoy a guilt-free special treat. Gooey sweets every now and then will not hurt me—provided I soon work off the calories. If I need to rationalize . . . well, I just say that I'm practicing carbohydrate-loading! Moderation is a key word when it comes to treats. The small ice cream cone generally satisfies my craving just as well as the humongous sundae!

Chapter 7
Soups

Be Creative

Soup can be a hearty meal in itself, an accompaniment to a sandwich, a light supper, or even a bedtime snack. In the wintertime, I enjoy soups as the mainstay of my diet. I'm usually creative when it comes to concocting them. Anything goes! Canned or dried soups—although loaded with sodium—are quick, easy, and readily available.

Here are some ways to convert plain ol' canned soup into an exotic treat:

- Combine soups: onion and chicken noodle
cream of tomato and vegetable

- Heat with milk (regular, powdered, or evaporated) for extra nutrition.

- Add ingredients: diced celery, broccoli, tomatoes, leftover casseroles, noodles, vegetables, diced meat, chopped nuts, or raisins

- Add seasonings: curry powder to chicken soup
  cloves to tomato soup
  wine, sherry, vermouth, to mushroom soup

- Add toppings: parmesan cheese
  grated cheddar
  cottage cheese
  sesame seeds
  croutons

- Make your own croutons: Spread margarine on sliced bread. Sprinkle with the seasonings of your choice: garlic salt, oregano, basil, parmesan cheese. Stack, cut into cubes. Distribute on a pie plate. Toast in the oven at 250°F. for 30 minutes.

- Bouillon or broth is a convenient soup base. I make a quick "vegetable-salad soup" by adding diced broccoli, celery, green peppers, spinach, and even lettuce to boiling broth. I cook it for 1 minute and it's ready—a nutritious, crunchy, Chinese-type soup. A tasty way to have a hot salad on a cold day!

Canned soups and bouillon do have a lot of heart-unhealthy salt. Making your own soup is easy as well as more healthful. Combine the ingredients, and let them cook while you go for your run. Dinner will be ready when you are! I save the cooking water from vegetables, keep it in a jar in my refrigerator and use it as a soup base. It is rich in vitamins B and C. On weekends, I make a big pot of soup that I enjoy for lunch or dinner the next week. I like hearty soups, such as split pea or lentil. I make them in large quantities, then freeze them in individual portions. (Cottage cheese containers are perfect.) They are handy meals all ready to heat and eat with a salad, some whole wheat crackers, and cheese.

I hope that you learn to be creative when making soups. This is your chance to clean out the refrigerator. For example, cook leftovers together with tired vegetables in a commercial onion soup base. Top with cheese. Voila!. . .a gourmet treat!

Recipes for Soups ▶

Homemade Chicken Soup
Carrot Soup
Fish and Broccoli Soup
Zucchini Soup
Lentil Soup
Egg Drop Soup
Quick Bean Soup
Tomato Soup with Veggies
Meaty French Onion Soup
Corn and 'Tater Soup

Homemade Chicken Soup

The kind that mother makes for curing all ailments.

1   large chicken, cut up
4   carrots, cut up
3   stalks celery, cut up
2   large onions, chopped
1   tbsp. salt
1/8   tsp. pepper

Optional:
   rice or noodles
   1   bay leaf
   1/8   tsp. thyme
   1   tsp. parsley

1.   Put chicken in a pot and cover with cold water.

2.   Add vegetables and spices.

3.   Simmer for 2 hours, skimming off the fat.

4.   Remove the chicken pieces. Cool. Take the meat from the bones and dice. Add back to the soup.

5.   Cook the rice in the skimmed broth while you cut up the chicken.

Yield: 8 servings.

Carrot Soup

A light soup that is perfect for an appetizer before a pasta meal. If you do not have a blender, simply grate the carrots and enjoy a chunkier soup.

1   onion, coarsely chopped
2   tbsp. margarine
1   1-lb. bag carrots, chopped
4   cups chicken broth, homemade, canned, or from
      bouillon cubes
1/8   tsp. nutmeg
1   tbsp. parsley
1   cup yogurt (or evaporated milk)

1.   In a large pot, sauté onion in margarine until it is soft.

2.   Add carrots, chicken broth, nutmeg, and parsley.

3.   Simmer for 30 minutes.

4.   Remove from heat. Puree in blender (in batches).

5.   Add 1 cup yogurt (or evaporated milk). Heat, but do not boil.

Yield: 4 servings.

Fish and Broccoli Soup

I like this because it is easy, delicious, slightly different, and low calorie. For a heartier soup, I add cooked rice, or convert it into a substantial meal by serving it with homemade bread or Syrian-Mushroom Toasties.

4   cups chicken broth (homemade, canned, or
    bouillon)
Optional: 4   tbsp. cornstarch mixed with a little
    cold water
½   lb. white fish
2   stalks broccoli, chopped

Optional:
    chopped scallions
    sesame oil
    cooked rice

1.   Heat chicken broth.

2.   Optional: to slightly thicken the broth, stir in cornstarch mixed with water.

3.   Cut fish into 1-inch chunks. Add to the broth, along with the chopped broccoli.

4.   Cook for 6 minutes.

5.   Optional: garnish with scallions and sesame oil.

Yield: 4 servings.

Zucchini Soup

You can change the character of this soup by putting it in the blender.

1 tbsp. margarine
1 small onion, chopped
1 clove garlic, minced or ¼ tsp. garlic powder
3 cups chicken broth, homemade, canned, or from
     bouillon cubes
1 lb. (2 medium) zucchini, thinly sliced
1 can evaporated milk, or 1½ cups yogurt

Optional: 1 tsp. curry

1. In a saucepan, sauté onion and garlic in margarine until tender.

2. Add chicken broth, zucchini and curry.

3. Cover. Bring to boil, then simmer for 15 minutes.

4. Add evaporated milk or yogurt. Heat, but do not boil.

Yield: 4 servings.

Lentil Soup

I make this soup in quantity, and freeze it in small portions. When I heat it up, I add fresh vegetables—such as chopped celery or broccoli—to add a crunchy texture.

Lentils are a good source of protein as well as carbo-hydrates. To get the most protein value eat this soup with bread and cheese, or milk. Or, complement the protein in the lentils by cooking them with 1 cup raw rice and 2 more cups of water.

2   cups (1 lb.) dried lentils
12 cups water
2   large onions, chopped
2   large carrots, chopped
1   clove garlic, crushed
1   tbsp. salt, or 5 beef bouillon cubes or 1 pkg. dried
     onion soup mix
black pepper (to taste)

Optional: your choice of:
    1 tbsp. curry or 1 tsp. ground cloves
    2 tbsp. Worchestershire sauce (use less salt)
    1 tbsp. molasses
    1 can tomato paste
    soup bones

1.   Combine all ingredients in a large pot.

2.   Cover. Bring to a boil; simmer for one hour.

Yield: 10 servings.

Egg Drop Soup

This is so easy ... and low calorie. It makes a nice lunch, or an appetizer to a light dinner. By adding spinach leaves, broccoli, bean sprouts, or other vegetables, you can increase the nutritional value.

1 cup chicken broth, homemade, canned, or from
    bouillon
2 tsp. cornstarch mixed with a little cold water
1 egg
dash soy sauce

Optional:
    spinach leaves
    chopped broccoli
    green pepper, chopped
    bean sprouts
    Chinese cabbage, shredded
    scallions, chopped
    cooked rice

1. Bring broth to a boil.

2. Stir in cornstarch to slightly thicken the broth. Meanwhile slightly beat the egg with soy sauce.

3. Stir the boiling soup quickly. While it swirls, slowly add the beaten egg. Remove from heat. Do not stir.

4. Add the vegetables. They will cook from the heat of the soup—crunchy, but warmed.

5. Serve immediately.

Yield: 1 serving.

Quick Bean Soup

An easy, hearty soup that goes well with grilled cheese sandwiches or a salad.

Beans are a good source of protein. One half cup has the equivalent in protein to one ounce of meat. The quality of this protein is enhanced when you eat it with a dairy product, such as cheese, yogurt, or milk, or with some bread or crackers.

1   1-lb. can baked beans
1   pkg. dried onion soup mix
1   8-oz. can tomato sauce or tomato soup
3   cups water

1.   Combine all ingredients. Cover, bring to boil and simmer for 20 minutes.

Yield: 4-6 servings.

Tomato Soup with Veggies

A quick 10-minute-dash dinner or lunch. You can vary the recipe with different soups, such as cream of mushroom or celery, and different vegetables. I generally add frozen mixed vegetables . . . they are nice and colorful!

1   can tomato soup
1   soup-can water
Vegetables, as desired: fresh, frozen, canned, or leftover cooked
parmesan cheese, grated

1.   Heat soup with water.

2.   Add vegetables. Cook until tender.

3.   Pour soup into bowls. Add grated cheese and serve.

Yield: 2 servings.

Meaty French Onion Soup

If you are a vegetarian, simply leave out the hamburger, or swap it for baked beans.

By serving this soup with spinach or fruit salad, you'll have a well balanced meal.

½ **lb. hamburger**
1   **pkg. dried onion soup mix**
3   **cups water**
4   **sl. of toast**
4   **oz. cheese, grated, Swiss or muenster**

1.   In a saucepan, brown the hamburger. Drain the grease.

2.   Add the soup mix and water. Cover. Bring to a boil, reduce heat, and simmer for 20 minutes.

3.   Serve into bowls. Top with a slice of toast. Garnish with grated cheese.

Yield: 4 servings.

Corn and 'Tater Soup

*This hearty soup is quick and tasty but high in sodium.
Canned soups are a convenient base, but they do have a
significant amount of salt. Therefore, I use them occasionally,
rather than as a mainstay of my diet.*

*This soup is nicely accompanied by spinach stuffing as
a side dish, or simply whole wheat bread. You can vary the
soups for a different flavor by using tomato or mushroom.
The fresh vegetables add color and "crunch".*

1   can condensed cream of potato soup
1   1-lb. can corn, regular or cream style
1½   cups milk
4   oz. cheddar cheese, cubed
black pepper to taste

Optional: Your choice of vegetables such as:
    1   stalk celery, chopped
    1   stalk broccoli, chopped
    1   cup green peas

1. Combine corn, soup, milk, and vegetables.

2. Heat. Stir in cheese until melted.

Yield: 4 bowls.

Chapter 8
Salads

Salads are great for busy people. Simply toss most any food into a bowl and you have a meal-in-a-hurry. When I get tired of the traditional lettuce, tomato, and cucumber salads, I add some excitement. Here are my suggestions:

sunflower seeds
slivered almonds
chopped walnuts
sesame seeds
alfalfa sprouts
wheat germ

pineapple chunks
orange sections
apple cubes
grapes
raisins

cooked vegetables:
  green beans
  beets
  potato

garbanzo beans
kidney beans
tofu
grated cheese
hard boiled egg

- Rub the inside of the salad bowl with a crushed garlic clove for a hint of flavor.

- Need only part of an onion? Save the root half; it will stay fresh longer.

- Make your own croutons by toasting stale bread in a 250°F. oven. (See Soup section, for more detailed directions.)

- Darker salad greens have more vitamins and minerals than do pale lettuces. A serving (100 gms.) of romaine has 18 milligrams of vitamin C, spinach has 50 milligrams, and iceberg lettuce has only 8 milligrams.

    Peeling vegetables is both a waste of time and nutrition. Vitamin C is stored directly under the skin of vegetables so if you peel the tomato you'll lose 75% of the vitamin C. The skins are also an excellent source of fiber. If you peel the cucumber you lose 60% of the fiber content.

Watching Your Weight?

"When I'm on a diet, I eat only a salad for lunch. I figure that I'm better off calorically with low-calorie lettuce than high-carbohydrate bread." Despite this change, gymnast Tom Klein didn't lose weight. And he couldn't understand why. "What do you put in your salad besides lettuce?" I asked. "I make it at a salad bar . . . I add just about everything but the kitchen sink." Tom's "diet" salad provided 800 calories, twice the amount of his usual peanut butter sandwich.

    "Low-calorie" salads may be fattening. I warn my patients to watch the amount of "goodies," such as cottage cheese, garbanzo beans, croutons, and bacon bits that you add. Salad dressing is loaded with calories, so don't drown

the lettuce! Dilute oil-based dressings with extra vinegar,
lemon juice, or water. Add milk or water to creamy types and
you'll enjoy the taste and the moistness without the extra
calories.

Salad base:	
¼ head lettuce	15 calories
½ cucumber	10
½ green pepper	10
1 small tomato	25
1 small carrot	25
5 mushrooms	15
	100

Toppings:	
½ cup cottage cheese	120 calories
1 oz. cheese, grated	100
sprinkling bacon bits	50
handful of croutons	100
3 tbsp. salad dressing	230
	600

Additional:
1 thick slice bread/butter   200 calories

If calories aren't your concern enjoy the luxury of a nice dressing. Choose olive oil for the finest flavor or safflower oil for a high polyunsaturated choice. Mix the oil in a 3-to-1 proportion with wine vinegar or lemon juice.

Vitamin E is found in many salad oils. One and one-half tablespoons of safflower oil will supply 15 milligrams (100% of the RDA) of this vitamin. I've met many hopeful athletes who take vitamin E supplements to improve their performance. They are wasting their money. All carefully controlled scientific studies to date indicate *no* benefit from additional E. The "E" stands for *extravagant expense* not *extra endurance.*

Vitamin E Supplements

	R.D.A.	(Cost in 1980)
Vitamin E capsule	260%	11¢
Wheat germ oil capsule	16%	7¢
Wheat germ oil, 1 tsp.	6%	17¢
Corn oil, 1¼ tbsp.	100%	3¢

Fiber in Vegetables

The fiber content of a salad is surprisingly low. Lettuce, celery, spinach, mushrooms, and onions are all low fiber foods. Add fiber by including sunflower seeds, sesame seeds, artichokes, and wheat germ. Eat a bran muffin, a slice of whole wheat bread, or a cup of split pea soup as an accompaniment, to help you obtain the daily recommended 5-6 grams of fiber.

Salad:
    ¼ head iceberg lettuce   .2 gm. fiber
    3 stalks celery   .3
    ½ cucumber, peeled   .3
    1 small tomato   .4

Total   1.2 gm. fiber

1 cup split pea soup   .5 gm.
1 small bran muffin   .7

Total   1.2 gm. fiber

1 sl. bran bread   .7 gm.
2 tbsp. peanut butter   .6

Total   1.3 gm. fiber

The Breakfast Cereal section has more information on high-fiber foods.

Recipes for Salads ▶

Chinese Cucumber Salad
Carrot-Raisin Salad
Tomato-Pepper Salad
Three Bean Salad
Spinach Salad
Pocket Salad
Apple-Carrot Salad
Fruit Salad
Fruit Slaw

Salad Dressings:
    French Dressing
    Yogurt Dressing
    Russian Dressing
    Zero-Calorie Dressing

Chinese Cucumber Salad

I like these cucumber slices for low-calorie appetizers. They are also a good crunchy contrast with noodle casseroles. The peels and seeds make cucumbers a high-fiber food.

1   cucumber, thinly sliced

Dressing:
   1   tbsp. soy sauce
   1   tsp. sugar
   1-3 tsp. oil
   ¼   cup red wine vinegar
   1   small onion, finely chopped

Optional: sesame seeds

1. Make dressing.

2. Pour over cucumber slices. Mix well, chill.

3. Optional: Garnish with sesame seeds.

Yield: 4 servings.

Carrot-Raisin Salad

Carrots are an excellent source of vitamin A. This vitamin helps your eyes adjust to the dark, as they do when you come indoors on a sunny day.

4   medium carrots, grated
½   cup raisins
½   cup walnuts, chopped
3   tbsp. orange juice

Optional:
    yogurt
    mayonnaise
    honey

1.   Grate carrots.

2.   Mix remaining ingredients; chill.

Yield: 4 servings.

Tomato-Pepper Salad

This colorful salad will supply 100% of the RDA for vitamins A and C. It attractively complements pale pasta and fish dishes.

3   large tomatoes, diced in ½-inch cubes
1   large green pepper, diced
¼   cup wine vinegar
2-3   tbsp. oil

Optional:
>   garlic powder
>   pepper
>   salt
>   basil
>   chopped onion

1. Mix tomatoes and peppers.

2. Add oil, vinegar, and seasonings.

3. Mix and chill until ready to serve.

Yield: 4 servings.

Three Bean Salad

This salad is best made the night before to allow the flavors to blend. When I have the time, I prefer to use frozen or fresh green and wax beans since they have less sodium than do the canned type.

1   16-oz. can wax beans
1   16-oz. can green beans
1   16-oz. can kidney beans
¼   cup sugar
½   cup cider vinegar
¼   cup oil
¼   cup onion, finely chopped

1. Drain beans and place in mixing bowl.

2. Add remaining ingredients. Toss.

3. Chill until ready to serve.

Yield: 8 servings.

Spinach Salad

Spinach is rich in many vitamins, especially A, C, and folic acid. Although it also has iron, the iron is bound, and is poorly absorbed from the digestive tract.

fresh spinach

Dressing:
2	tbsp. orange juice
2	tbsp. wine vinegar
¼-½	cup oil

Optional toppings:
>   orange sections
>   toasted, slivered almonds
>   chopped hard-boiled egg

1. Wash spinach. Remove tough stems.

2. Mix dressing. Pour over spinach. Toss well.

3. Garnish with toppings.

Yield: 4 servings.

Pocket Salad

Eat as a salad or as a filling for a Syrian-Bread Pocket Sandwich.

Your choice of:
    finely chopped lettuce, green pepper, onion, tomato
    grated cheese
    cottage cheese
    parmesan cheese
    chopped egg
    flaked tuna
    mayonnaise or yogurt
    vinegar
    mustard
    curry
    garlic powder

1. Mix together any desired combination of finely chopped veggies and cheeses, egg, or tuna.

2. Make a salad dressing with any combination of the seasonings.

3. Stuff into pocket bread.

Apple-Carrot Salad

I like this for pot-luck suppers, as a change from cole slaw and tossed salads. It goes nicely with casserole-type meals.

1   apple, diced
1   carrot, grated
1   stalk celery, diced
½ cup raisins
¼ cup yogurt, mayonnaise or a combination
1   tbsp. orange juice
dash cinnamon

Optional:
    ¼ cup sunflower seeds
    ¼ cup walnuts, chopped
    1 tbsp. honey or sugar

1. In a large bowl, mix yogurt, mayonnaise, orange juice, and cinnamon.

2. Add fruits and vegetables.

3. Gently mix; chill.

Yield: 4 servings.

Fruit Salad

Combine fresh, frozen, canned, and dried fruits for a varied salad. I serve this in place of a vegetable or for dessert.

Dressing:
  ¾ cup yogurt, mayonnaise, or a combination
  ¼ cup orange juice
  dash cinnamon

Optional:
  nutmeg
  grated orange rind
  wine, brandy, or liqueur

Your choice of chopped:

apple	pineapple	strawberries
orange	raisins	blueberries
grapefruit	coconut	cantaloupe
banana	walnuts	watermelon
peach	sunflower	honeydew
pear	seeds	melon

1. Combine dressing ingredients. Gently mix with cut up fruits.

Yield: The dressing is sufficient for 3–4 cups of chopped fruit.

Fruit Slaw

Cabbage is an excellent source of vitamin C. One cup will provide 100% of the RDA.

2   cups cabbage, finely shredded
¼   cup pineapple pieces
1   orange, sectioned
1   red apple, chopped
2   tbsp. nuts, chopped
½   cup yogurt, mayonnaise, or a combination
¼   cup fruit juice

1. Mix cabbage and fruit.

2. Combine yogurt with fruit juice. Pour over fruit mixture.

Yield: 4 servings.

Salad Dressings

Olive oil is the first choice for salad dressings. However, since it is expensive, safflower oil is the best second choice. (Safflower oil is also highly polyunsaturated . . . a heart-healthy choice. Olive oil is monounsaturated and "neutral". It is neither beneficial nor harmful in the battle against heart disease.)

- *Wine vinegar, lemon juice, or combinations of the two, are the best sour accompaniment to the oil.*
- *Since salt and vinegar release the juices from the salad vegetables you should add the dressing as near to serving time as possible. This will prevent a wilted and soggy salad.*
- *Serve the salad dressing at room temperature. It will spread further and coat the greens more evenly.*
- *Yogurt makes an excellent low-calorie and low-fat replacement for mayonnaise.*

French Dressing

2	tbsp. lemon juice
2	tbsp. wine vinegar
½-¾	cup oil
½	tsp. paprika
½	tsp. dry mustard
½	tsp. salt
1	tsp. sugar

dash cayenne pepper

1. Combine all ingredients in a jar with a tightly fitting lid. Shake well before serving.

Yield: 1 cup.

Yogurt Dressing

This has half the calories of regular dressings, which contain more oil or mayonnaise.

¼ cup yogurt, plain
¼ cup mayonnaise
¼ cup wine vinegar
2 tbsp. orange juice
dash garlic salt
black pepper

Optional:
   ½ tsp. basil
   pinch celery seed
   ¼ tsp. parsley

1. Combine ingredients well. Chill.

Yield: 1 cup.

Russian Dressing

For weight-watchers, yogurt is the low-calorie substitute for mayonnaise.
   I like this dressing on salads topped with cottage cheese.

½ cup mayonnaise, yogurt, or a combination
½ cup catsup or chili sauce

Optional: sweet relish

1. Combine ingredients and chill.

Yield: 1 cup.

Zero-Calorie Dressing

Great for weight watchers!

½ cup tomato juice
2 tbsp. lemon juice or vinegar
1 tbsp. onion, finely chopped
pepper
salt

Optional:
    parsley
    mustard
    garlic
    horseradish
    herbs

1. Combine ingredients in a jar with a tightly fitted cap. Shake well betore serving.

Yield: 3/4 cup.

Chapter 9

Breads

If you think bread is just an inexpensive filler you're wrong. Bread is a nutritious part of the athlete's diet. In addition to supplying energy for your muscles, enriched whole wheat and dark breads supply B-vitamins, iron, fiber, potassium, vitamin E, zinc, and other trace minerals. B-vitamins are especially important for athletes since they help to convert the foods you eat into energy.

White vs. Dark—Enriched vs. "All natural"

White bread is not a junk food. Even the fluffy commercial product has some nutritional value. Dark bread *is* better however, because it is less processed. When wheat is processed into white flour, many nutrients are removed along with the bran and wheat germ. At least four—thiamin, niacin, riboflavin, and iron—are generally added back to the flour. Enriched white bread may actually have a higher content of these four nutrients than whole wheat bread. However, it will lack the many other trace elements and fiber that were removed but were not replaced. Processing reduces the nutritional value of wheat, by removing the bran and the germ. Even some whole wheat flours are processed and have fewer nutrients (referred to as "extraction" in the chart).

	mg. Iron	mg. Potassium	mg. Thiamin	mg. [1] Niacin
100 gm:				
Wheat bran (approx. 10 tbsp.)	14.5	1,120	.720	21.0
Wheat germ (10 tbsp.)	9.5	825	2,010	4.0
Flour, whole wheat (approx. 1 cup)	3.5	370	.550	4.5
Flour, 80% extraction	1.5	95	.260	2.0
Flour, white (approx. 1 cup)	1.0	95	.060	1.0
Flour, enriched	3.0	95	.440	3.5
Recommended Daily Allowance	10(men) 18(women)	2500	1500	20.0

Many French, Italian, and Syrian breads are not enriched. Dark breads such as whole wheat, rye, sprouted wheat, bran, and pumpernickel are better choices. *Enriched* dark breads are the best choice. Read the bread label. Look for the word "enriched" among the ingredients or for a list of

---

[1] Source: B. Walt and A. Merrill. "Composition of Foods: raw, processed, prepared." *Agriculture Handbook No. 8*, U.S. Government Printing Office, Washington, D. C., 1963.

---

chemically-sounding names such as ferrous sulfate (iron), thiamine hydrochloride (B_1), niacin, and riboflavin (B_2).

Natural breads with "no additives" have no beneficial iron or B-vitamins added to them. Athletes want these additives. For example, iron is the part of hemoglobin in the red blood cell that carries oxygen from the lungs to the working muscles. An iron-deficient diet, common among women athletes, may result in anemia with symptoms of fatigue and a run-down feeling. You won't be able to perform at your best without adequate amounts of iron.

I counsel many struggling weight-watchers who avoid

Nutritional Value: Fat vs. Carbohydrate

1 tbsp. margarine		2 sl. wheat bread (enriched)
Calories	100	190
Carbohydrate	0	75% of the calories
Fat	100% of the calories	14% of the calories
Protein	0	11 gm.
Vitamin A	10% of the RDA	0% of the RDA
Vitamin C	0	0
Thiamin	0	0
Thiamin	0	10
Riboflavin	0	10
Niacin	0	6
Niacin	0	8
Calcium	0	0
Iron	0	8

Based on: J. Pennington and H. Church. *Bowes and Church's Food Values of Portions Commonly Used.* Harper and Row, Publishers, N.Y., 1980.

breads, because they've been brainwashed to think that carbohydrates are fattening. They are mistaken! Breads and other starches (in reasonable amounts) are *not* fattening. The butter, margarine, mayonnaise, and peanut butter that you eat with them *are* fattening. For example:

6 saltines	70 calories
1 tbsp. peanut butter	100
1 medium baked potato	80
3 tbsp. soured cream	90

If you diet by giving up high carbohydrate foods, such as bread, pasta, and crackers, you are actually giving up the fattening fats which you put on these carbohydrates, such as the butter on the bread. Fat has very few vitamins. You'd be wiser to eat the nutritious carbohydrates and give up only the fats. (In the section "Are You Becoming an Abdominal Snowman" I will say more about healthful weight loss suggestions.)

Good Additives

The following list shows you that many of the technical sounding words you see on food labels are simply vitamins and minerals that are added for your health.

Nutrient	Additive Name
Vitamin A	beta carotene vitamin A palmitate
Vitamin B_1	thiamin thiamine hydrochloride thiamine mononitrate
Vitamin B_2	riboflavin
Vitamin B_6	pyridoxine hydrochloride
Vitamin B_{12}	cobalamin concentrate cyanocobalamin
Vitamin C	ascorbic acid sodium ascorbate
Vitamin D	calciferol ergocalciferol cholecalciferol
Vitamin E	alpha tocopherol mixed alpha tocopherols concentrate alpha tocopheryl acetate alpha tocopheryl acetate concentrate alpha tocopheryl acid succinate
Folic Acid	folic acid folacin
Vitamin K	phytonadione
Niacin	niacin niacinamide

Nutrient	Additive Name
Calcium	calcium carbonate
	calcium glycerophosphate
	calcium phosphate
	calcium pyrophosphate
	calcium sulfate
Copper	copper gluconate
	cupric sulfate
Iodine	iodized salt
Iron	ferric phosphate
	iron phosphate
	ferric orthophosphate
	sodium ferric pyrophosphate
	ferric pyrophosphate
	iron pyrophosphate
	ferrous furmarate
	ferrous gluconate
	ferrous sulfate
	electrolytic iron
	reduced iron
Magnesium	magnesium phosphate
	magnesium sulfate
Phosphorus	calcium phosphate
	sodium phosphate
	sodium pyrophosphate
Potassium	potassium chloride
	potassium glycerophosphate
	potassium iodide
Sodium	iodized salt
Zinc	zinc oxide
	zinc sulfate

Source: Heslin, J. *No-Nonsense Nutrition.* CBI Publishing Co., Inc., Boston, MA., 1978.

Recipes for Breads ►

Apricot Bread
Banana Bread
Date-Nut Bread
Zucchini Bread
Whole Wheat-Raisin Quick Bread
Peanut Butter Bread
Crunchy Corn Bread
English Tea Biscuits
Bran Muffins
Blueberry Muffins
Parmesan-Garlic Bread
Herbed French Bread
Syrian Bread-Mushroom Toasties

Basic Yeast Bread
Oatmeal Bread

Quick Breads and Muffins

The secret for light and fluffy quick breads, muffins, and biscuits is: **Stir the flour in lightly,** *and stir only 20 seconds. Ignore the lumps! If you beat the batter too much the gluten (protein) in the flour will develop and toughen the dough.*

Most of the recipes do not specify the type of flour. You can use whole wheat, enriched white, or a combination. I generally prefer half- and half. Whole wheat is the most nutritious, since it contains the fiber, trace minerals, and vitamins that are removed from the refined flours. However, too much whole wheat flour results in a heavy baked product. For best results, substitute 3/4 cup whole wheat flour for 1 cup white all-purpose flour.

Have you ever wondered how baked goods rise? Quick breads are generally leavened by baking soda and/or baking powder. Baking soda (an alkaline substance) reacts with moisture and an acid—baking powder, brown sugar, molasses, honey, fruit juice—to form bubbles of carbon dioxide in the batter. Baking powder reacts with moisture and heat. In the hot oven, the bubbles expand and cause the batter to rise.

If you exchange white sugar for honey, brown sugar, or molasses you should use only ½ teaspoon baking powder per two cups flour, and add ½ teaspoon baking soda to neutralize the acids. Otherwise, the final product may have an off-taste.

Most cookbooks instruct you to sift together the baking powder and flour. This method produces the best results. In some of these recipes, I direct you to mix the baking powder in with the wet ingredients, and gently add the flour last. My method is easier and produces an acceptable product. Although this product might be slightly heavier to the eyes of a perfectionist, I prefer to save the time and energy ... and I pass the tip on to you.

To prevent breads and cakes from sticking I place a piece of waxed paper in the baking pan before I pour the *batter. For me, this works better than greasing the pan. After the bread has baked, I let it cool for five minutes then tip it out of the pan, and peel off the paper.*

When I'm in a hurry, I bake the quick breads in a 9-inch x 9-inch square pan, instead of in a loaf. They bake in half the time. I also bake muffin batter in a 9-inch x 9-inch pan. It's easier and eliminates the hard-to-wash muffin tin.

Apricot Bread

For variety, try cranberries instead of apricots. Or, exchange one half of the milk for orange juice; add ½ tsp. baking soda.

1½	cups flour
½	cup sugar
1	tsp. salt
½	tsp. baking powder
¾	cup Grape-nuts
2/3	cup dried apricots, chopped
1	cup milk
1	egg
¼	cup oil

1. Preheat oven to 350°F.

2. In a bowl, mix flour, sugar, salt, and baking powder. Stir in Grape-nuts and apricots.

3. Mix together milk, egg, and oil.

4. Add to flour mixture. Stir 20 seconds, or until just moistened.

5. Pour into greased loaf pan. Bake for 60 minutes, or until toothpick inserted near the center comes out clean.

Yield: 1 loaf.

Banana Bread

For best results, use very ripe bananas that are covered with brown speckles.

Bananas are potassium-rich—a good way to replace the potassium lost with sweating.

When I'm hiking I make banana bread sandwiches with peanut butter and honey . . . my favorite high-energy foods!

3	large, ripe bananas
1	egg
2	tbsp. oil
¼	cup milk
¼-½	cup sugar
1	tsp. salt
1	tsp. baking soda
½	tsp. baking powder
1½	cups flour

1. Preheat oven to 350°F.

2. Mash bananas with a fork.

3. Add egg, oil, milk, sugar, salt, baking powder and soda. Beat well.

4. Gently blend flour into the banana mixture, stir 20 seconds, or until moistened.

5. Pour into greased or wax-papered loaf pan.

6. Bake for 45 minutes or until toothpick inserted near the middle comes out clean.

Yield: 1 loaf.

Date-Nut Bread

This has always been a favorite at Christmas time. I enjoy it with low-fat cream cheese or peanut butter. For variety, I sometimes add sunflower seeds instead of the chopped nuts.

8	oz. dates, chopped
1½	cups boiling water
2	tbsp. oil
1	egg
½-1	cup sugar
½	cup walnuts, chopped
1	tsp. salt
2	tsp. baking soda
2½	cups flour

1. Put dates in a bowl and pour boiling water over them. Let stand until cool. (I put them in the refrigerator for 5-10 minutes.)

2. Preheat oven to 350°F.

3. Add oil, egg, sugar, salt, walnuts to the dates; beat well.

4. Combine the baking soda and flour. Gently stir into the date mixture.

5. Pour into greased or wax-papered pan. Bake for 45-60 minutes, or until toothpick inserted near center comes out clean.

Yield: 1 loaf.

Zucchini Bread

You can vary this recipe with carrots or cucumber instead of zucchini. Add your choice of dried fruits, coconut, or brown sugar.

1½	cups zucchini, grated
2	eggs
½	cup oil
½-¾	cup sugar
½	tsp. salt
½	tsp. cinnamon
½	tsp. baking powder
½	tsp. baking soda
1½	cups flour

Optional:

½	cup nuts, chopped
½	cup raisins

1. Preheat oven to 350°F.

2. Mix all ingredients except flour. Beat well.

3. Gently add flour to zucchini mixture, stirring just until blended.

4. Pour into greased or wax-papered loaf pan. Bake for about 60 minutes, or until toothpick inserted near the center comes out clean.

Yield: 1 loaf.

Whole Wheat-Raisin Quick Bread

I frequently enjoy this bread with a bowl of hearty soup . . . a satisfying winter-time supper.

1½	cup milk
2	tbsp. vinegar
½	cup molasses
½	cup sugar
¼	cup oil
½	cup raisins
1	tsp. salt
1½	tsp. baking soda
1½	tsp. baking powder
½	cup white flour
2½	cup whole wheat flour

1. Preheat oven to 350°F.

2. In a bowl, make soured milk by mixing milk and vinegar. Let stand a minute.

3. Mix together remaining ingredients, except for flour. Beat well.

4. Gently add flour, stirring just until blended.

5. Pour into greased or wax-papered bread pan.

6. Bake for one hour, or until toothpick inserted near center comes out clean.

Yield: 1 loaf.

Peanut Butter Bread

This bread is great toasted for breakfast. For variety, try adding a mashed banana (reduce the milk by ¼ cup).

2	cups flour
4	tsp. baking powder
½	tsp. salt
1/3	cup sugar
¾	cup peanut butter
1¼	cup milk
1	egg

1. Preheat oven to 350°F.

2. In a bowl, mix together flour, baking powder, salt, and sugar.

3. Cut in peanut butter with two knives (scissor style) until crumbly.

4. Lightly stir egg and milk into the flour mixture.

5. Pour into greased or wax-papered loaf pan.

6. Bake for 55–50 minutes, or until toothpick inserted near center comes out clean.

Yield: 1 loaf.

Crunchy Corn Bread

The sesame seeds complement the protein from the cornmeal, making this bread high in nutritional value. Excellent when served with chili or soups.

¾ cup whole wheat flour
½ cup white flour
¾ cup cornmeal
3 tbsp. sesame seeds
3 tbsp. sugar
5 (yes, 5)   tsp. baking powder
1 tsp. salt
1 egg
1 cup milk
2 tbsp. oil

1. Preheat oven to 375°F.

2. Mix dry ingredients.

3. Beat egg with milk and oil. Add to dry ingredients.

4. Spoon batter into greased or wax-papered 9-inch square or round pan.

5. Bake for 30–35 minutes, or until toothpick inserted near center comes out clean.

Yield: 9 servings.

English Tea Biscuits

These simple but crunchy biscuits are nice for breakfast, brunch, or carbohydrate loading, especially when complemented with jelly or honey. For a substantial breakfast, serve them with ricotta cheese and strawberry jam.

½   cup milk
½   cup sugar
1   tsp. baking soda
½   cup oil
2¼   cups white flour
1   cup whole wheat flour
¾   cup oatmeal (uncooked)
1½   tsp. salt

Optional: 1 tsp. cinnamon

1.   Preheat oven to 400°F.

2.   Put milk, oil, and sugar in a sauce pan. Bring to a boil. Remove from heat and add baking soda. Stir until dissolved. Cool.

3.   Combine flour, oats, and salt in bowl.

4.   Add milk mixture. Stir lightly until dry ingredients are moistened.

5.   Dust your fingers with flour, then shape dough into round biscuits (½-inch thick x 3-inch diameter).

6.   Place on ungreased cookie sheet. Bake 10-12 minutes, or until golden.

Yield: 15 biscuits.

Bran Muffins

These muffins are tasty not only at breakfast, but also with lunch. Spread with peanut butter for dinner in place of bread. They are a good source of fiber and carbohydrates.

2½	cups 40% Bran Flakes or Raisin Bran
1	cup milk
1	egg
¼	cup oil
¼-½	cup sugar
½	tsp. salt
1	tbsp. baking powder
1	cup flour

Optional—your choice of:

½	cup raisins
½	cup sunflower seeds
½	cup nuts, chopped
¼	cup wheat germ
1	cup apple, chopped
1	cup cranberries, chopped
1	tsp. vanilla
½	tsp. cinnamon

1. Preheat oven to 400°F.

2. In a bowl, combine Bran Flakes with milk. Let stand for 1 to 2 minutes, until the cereal is softened.

3. Add oil, egg, sugar, salt, and baking powder. Mix well.

4. Gently stir in flour, mixing only until combined.

5. Portion into greased muffin tins.

6. Bake about 25 minutes, or until golden.

Yield: 1 dozen.

Blueberry Muffins

These muffins could be filed under desserts. They're sweet and delicious. If you prefer, bake them in a 9-inch x 9-inch cake pan to make a coffee cake.

Apart from the fiber content, blueberries have insignificant nutritional value. They are a low-calorie, flavorful treat for weight watchers.

½ cup margarine
1 cup sugar
2 eggs
2 tsp. baking powder
1 tsp. salt
½ cup milk
2 cups flour
2 cups blueberries

1. Preheat oven to 375°F.

2. Cream margarine with sugar.

3. Beat in eggs.

4. Add baking powder, salt, and milk. Beat well.

5. Gently stir in flour, then blueberries.

6. Fill muffin cups 2/3 full. Sprinkle with sugar if desired.

7. Bake for 25–35 minutes. Let cool in the pan.

Yield: 12 muffins.

Parmesan-Garlic Bread

This bread is good served with spaghetti, soup, or salads.

Syrian Bread
margarine
garlic powder
parmesan cheese
parsley flakes

1. Mix margarine and garlic powder.

2. Separate Syrian bread into circles and spread with margarine.

3. Sprinkle with parmesan cheese and parsley flakes.

4. Broil until golden and bubbly.

Herbed French Bread

The tasty margarine for this bread may also be used to flavor vegetables.

1   **stick margarine, softened**
½   **tsp. oregano**
¼   **tsp. basil**
⅛   **tsp. garlic powder**
1   **loaf French bread**

1. Blend all ingredients together.

2. Cut French bread diagonally into 1½-inch slices.

3. Spread margarine mix on both sides of each slice.

4. Wrap tightly in aluminum foil.

5. Bake 375°F. for 25 minutes or until hot.

Yield: 8-10 servings.

Syrian Bread-Mushroom Toasties

These toasties go well with eggs (such as Stove-Top Broccoli Souffle), and soup. I sometimes make them for appetizers.

2   loaves Syrian bread
1   3-oz. pkg. cream cheese, softened

1   tbsp. margarine
12   oz. fresh mushrooms, sliced,
      or 8-oz. can mushrooms
1   small onion, finely diced

¼   tsp. garlic powder
2   tsp. Worchestershire sauce
¼   cup parmesan cheese

1. In skillet, sauté for 5 minutes the onion, mushrooms, and garlic powder in the margarine.

2. Add Worchestershire and cook until the liquid evaporates.

3. Cut open the Syrian bread into circles and spread it with cream cheese.

4. Top with the mushroom mixture; sprinkle with parmesan cheese.

5. Place on a cookie sheet. Bake at 325°F. for 10 minutes or until toasted.

Yield: 4 servings.

Yeast Breads

If you have never made your own yeast bread don't be afraid to give it a try. Among other things kneading the dough is good upper-body exercise and will help to build strong arm muscles. While the dough rises you can go for a nice run.

Bake the bread while you stretch and change your clothes, and then share the tempting treat with your training partner while it's still warm from the oven. You'll never lack for people with whom to run!

The only trick to making yeast bread is to soak the yeast in warm water that feels comfortable to your fingertips. If you use hot water you'll scald the living yeast to death, and the bread won't rise. In such a case, I bake the dough, slice it very thinly, and pass it off for a heavy European bread! Most yeast bread recipes instruct you to let the dough rise twice— once in a bowl, once in the pan. I generally let it rise only once—in the pan. This results in a heavier, coarser bread, but I like it that way, and also I like saving the extra time. Bread dough can be frozen. When making bread, I usually double the recipe. I flatten the extra dough into discs, wrap it loosely, and freeze it. Since my first mistake, I now remember to unwrap it before thawing the dough.

Basic Yeast Bread

This is the simplest of yeast breads . . . a good place for new bakers to start! The recipe comes out nicely with half white and half whole wheat flour.

Homemade bread is a treat for carbohydrate-loaders. Serve with a hearty bean soup, and you have a high carbohydrate, low fat meal.

2	cups hot tap water
1	pkg. yeast
1	tbsp. sugar or honey
1	tbsp. salt
4-5	cups flour

1. Put 2 cups of water into a large bowl. The water should feel warm to your fingertips. Add the yeast.

2. Add the sugar, salt, and 1 cup flour; mix.

3. Add another 1½ cups flour; mix.

4. Gradually add the remaining flour. When you can no longer stir the dough pour it onto a floured counter and knead it well . . . about 10 minutes.

5. When the dough is smooth and elastic shape it into a round or long loaf and place it on a greased baking sheet.

6. Cover loosely with plastic wrap. Let rise until almost double.

7. Bake at 350°F. for 45-60 minutes, or until it sounds hollow when tapped with your fingers.

Yield: 1 large loaf.

Oatmeal Yeast Bread

I usually make lentil soup at the same time I make yeast bread. The combination is deliciously rewarding, and nutritionally excellent for athletes who want high carbohydrate, low fat meals. I use a combination of half white and half whole wheat flour in this recipe. The bread comes out wholesome, but not overwhelmingly solid.

I divide the dough in half, making one loaf with raisins and the other with sesame seeds.

4	cups hot tap water
2	pkgs. yeast
½	cup molasses or honey
2	tbsp. sugar
¼	cup oil
1	tbsp. salt
1½	cup oatmeal, uncooked
8	cups flour

Optional—your choice of:

½	cup bran
½	cup wheat germ
½	Wheatena
½	cup sesame seeds
1	cup raisins
2	tsp. cinnamon

1. Put 4 cups of water into a large bowl. The water should feel warm to your fingertips. Add the yeast.

2. Combine the remaining ingredients, adding 2 cups of flour to start; mix well.

3. Stir in 4 cups flour, then gradually add more. When you can no longer stir in the flour pour the dough onto a floured counter top and knead it well . . . about 10 minutes, or until it is smooth and elastic.

4. Shape it into loaves and place in greased pans. Cover loosely with plastic wrap. Let rise until almost double.

5. Bake 350°F. for 45-60 minutes, or until it sounds hollow when tapped with your fingers.

6. Let cool at least ten minutes before slicing!

Yield: 2 large loaves.

Chapter 10

Protein: How Much Meat Should The Athlete Eat?

Everyone knows that as an athlete you need to fortify your body with extra protein . . . right? WRONG! Research studies have indicated that the competitive cross-country skier has the same needs during exercise while at rest. Exercise does not increase your daily protein requirement. Exercise does, however, increase your need for calories from carbohydrates.

I recommend that you feast on bread and bananas rather than steak and eggs. Carbohydrate foods cost less than meats, are excellent sources of vitamins and minerals, and are better utilized by the muscles for optimal athletic performance.

The main function of protein is to build body tissue. Since the typical American diet provides two to three times the daily amount recommended for protein, the extra is converted into energy. Hence, meat is a very expensive energy source. It is also high in fat and cholesterol, both of which are linked with heart disease. I recommend that the health-conscious athlete or exerciser choose carbohydrates

---

How Much Protein Do You Need?

For a 150-pound male, the recommended daily allowance is 56 grams, which can be obtained from the following foods:

	grams protein
2 glasses of milk	16
4 oz. of meat, fish, poultry, or cheese	28
Additional food (bread, cereal, vegetables)	12
	56

One pound of muscle tissue contains:

0.22 lb. protein
0.06 lb. fat
0.72 lb. water

1.00 lb. muscle tissue is equivalent to
600 calories of energy

Source: E. Darden. "Gaining Body Weight." *Nautilus Magazine,*
Vol. 1, Summer, 1980.

as the dietary mainstay. Meat should be a secondary source of calories. Bread, cereal, pasta, fruit, juice, vegetables, and other carbohydrate foods are the better fuel for your muscles. You do not need to eat red meats—hamburger, pork chops, steak, roast lamb—to have a well-balanced diet. These are heart-unhealthy. Secondly, they are harder to digest than carbohydrates. Fish, chicken, and turkey are lower in fat and

are healthier choices. Vegetarian athletes who carefully select the right combination of nuts, beans, peas, and grains consume a sufficient diet. The thoroughbred race horse is one example of a top athlete that maintains strength and stamina with a pure vegetarian diet. In the section, "The Vegetarian Athlete," I will explain more about meatless diets.

Special protein supplements that claim to produce high energy, stamina, and strength are unnecessary items in your diet. Training and regular exercise rather than meat and eggs will improve your athletic skill.

The key to developing muscular bulk is repeated hard exercise that stresses the muscle. For example, weightlifting—a resistence exercise—builds muscle bulk. Running, on the other hand, develops leaner muscles.

Do you eat too much protein?

You are flushing away your food budget if you are an average American who consumes two to three times your body's need for protein. Extra protein is not stored in your body, but rather is converted into energy. Urea, the waste product formed in the conversion, is carried by the blood to your kidneys. You flush it down the toilet. Carbohydrates and fats, more efficient energy sources, do not contribute to urea formation.

Many of my patients want to know how much protein they actually need. I easily calculate this and you can too. Simply multiply your weight in pounds by 0.4 if you are an adult; by 0.45 if you are a growing adolescent. For example, I weigh 110 pounds. I multiply 110 pounds by 0.4 grams protein per pound. The answer, 44 grams of protein, is my recommended daily allowance. This figure is based on the needs of the "average person." We each have slightly different needs—some higher, some lower—due to our particular metabolism. The National Research Council, which establishes the RDA, adds a generous (100%) margin of safety to compensate for these individual variations. Hence, the RDA is appropriate even for weight-lifters, who are increasing muscle bulk.

Now, to determine the amount of protein that you eat in a day: write down everything you ate and drank in the past

twenty-four hours. You can use the following guidelines to estimate the protein content of your diet. Simply write down the number of grams of protein in each food item according to the serving size, then total them up. The figure that you calculate will be a rough estimate but, nevertheless will give you a general indication of your protein intake. If you eat more protein than you need, I encourage you to eat less meat and instead, invest the savings in more fruits and vegetables.

Average protein content of some basic foods:

Meat and high protein foods: 7 grams per:
   1 oz. meat, fish, and poultry
   1 egg
   1 sl. bologna, luncheon meat
   ¼ cup tuna fish
   ½ cup baked beans, lentils, dried peas
   2 tbsp. peanut butter
   24 walnut halves

Dairy products: 8 grams per:
   8 oz. milk
   1 cup yogurt
   1 oz. cheese
   1/3 cup cottage cheese
   2 cups ice cream

Bread and cereals: 2 grams per:
   1 sl. bread
   ½ cup rice, noodles, pasta, potato

Starchy vegetables: 2 grams per:
   ½ cup peas, carrots, beets, winter squash

Fruits, vegetables, and juices:
   Most contain only small amounts, which may
   contribute a total of 5 to 10 grams,
   depending on the quantity eaten.

Butter, margarine, oil, sugar, candy, coffee, tonic, and alcohol contain no protein.

Cakes, cookies, pies, and other sweets have small amounts of protein.

What about cholesterol?

In my practice I repeatedly answer some basic questions. A typical example is, "Should I stop eating red meat and eggs?" My patients are confused about the conflicting reports regarding diet, blood cholesterol, and heart disease.

The cholesterol controversy—whether the cholesterol you eat influences the level of cholesterol in your blood—remains unresolved. However, the following facts tell a true story:

1. Eating a high cholesterol diet (eggs, shrimp, liver) usually causes high blood cholesterol.

2. Even with a low cholesterol diet, your body can produce excessive amounts of cholesterol as long as your diet is high in saturated fats as butter, beef, pork, soured cream, and gravy.

3. When your diet is low in the saturated animal fats but high in polyunsaturated fat (corn oil margarine, vegetable oils) the blood cholesterol drops.

4. A high level of blood cholesterol is linked with arteriosclerosis. The cholesterol accumulates in the walls of the blood vessels throughout the body, especially those in the heart. This build-up limits blood flow to the heart muscle and contributes to heart attacks.

5. Athletes frequently have greater amounts of a "good" cholesterol—HDL—which transports the "bad" cholesterol out of your body. What foods have the most cholesterol? Most animal proteins (meat, fish, and poultry) have similar

amounts of cholesterol with the exception of eggs, liver, and shrimp.

Cholesterol content:	mg./3½ oz.
tuna, haddock	60
chicken, turkey, light meat	60
chicken, turkey, dark meat	70
beef, pork, lamb	70
cheese, cheddar	105
shrimp	150
egg (one medium)	250
liver, calve's	440
Recommended maximum:	300 mg./day

What foods have the most saturated fat? Meats and protein foods vary in their fat content. For example, hamburger obviously has more fat than fish. Beef, pork, and lamb are high in saturated fat as compared to chicken or fish. You eat saturated fats in cheese, milk, ice cream, as well as coffee creamer, cookies, butter, inexpensive margarines, and processed peanut butter. All of these foods will contribute to high blood cholesterol even if you eat low cholesterol foods.

What foods have the most polyunsaturated fats? Liquid vegetable oils are the best source of polyunsaturated fats. Use them in salad dressings, cooking, sauteeing, and baking. When you buy margarine choose the brand with the word "liquid" as the first ingredient. Healthful polyunsaturated fats to include in your diet are (in order of preference):

safflower oil	74% polyunsaturated
sunflower oil	64%
corn oil	58%
soybean oil	57%

Definitions: Fat and Cholesterol

Fatty acids are grouped in three families:

> saturated
> monosaturated
> polyunsaturated

Each fatty acid molecule consists of atoms of carbon, hydrogen, and oxygen arranged in a specific pattern.

When there is a hydrogen at every available spot in the molecule, the fatty acid is saturated. It is holding all the hydrogen that is possible; its chemical structure looks like this:

$$R-\overset{\overset{\displaystyle H}{|}}{\underset{\underset{\displaystyle H}{|}}{C}}-\overset{\overset{\displaystyle H}{|}}{\underset{\underset{\displaystyle H}{|}}{C}}-\overset{\overset{\displaystyle H}{|}}{\underset{\underset{\displaystyle H}{|}}{C}}-\overset{\overset{\displaystyle H}{|}}{\underset{\underset{\displaystyle H}{|}}{C}}-\overset{\overset{\displaystyle H}{|}}{\underset{\underset{\displaystyle H}{|}}{C}}-\overset{\displaystyle OH}{\underset{}{C}}=O$$

When some hydrogen is missing, the molecule is not saturated; it is unsaturated. If just one molecule of hydrogen is missing, the fatty acid is monosaturated. Olive oil is a monosaturated fat.

$$R-\overset{\displaystyle H}{C}=\overset{\displaystyle H}{C}-\overset{\overset{\displaystyle H}{|}}{\underset{\underset{\displaystyle H}{|}}{C}}-\overset{\overset{\displaystyle H}{|}}{\underset{\underset{\displaystyle H}{|}}{C}}-\overset{\overset{\displaystyle H}{|}}{\underset{\underset{\displaystyle H}{|}}{C}}-\overset{\overset{\displaystyle H}{|}}{\underset{\underset{\displaystyle H}{|}}{C}}-\overset{\displaystyle OH}{C}=O$$

If two or more molecules of hydrogen are missing, the molecule is polyunsaturated. Corn oil is a polyunsaturated fat.

$$R-\overset{\displaystyle H}{C}=\overset{\displaystyle H}{C}-\overset{\overset{\displaystyle H}{|}}{\underset{\underset{\displaystyle H}{|}}{C}}-\overset{\overset{\displaystyle H}{|}}{\underset{}{C}}-\overset{\displaystyle H}{C}=\overset{\displaystyle H}{C}-\overset{\overset{\displaystyle H}{|}}{\underset{\underset{\displaystyle H}{|}}{C}}-\overset{\displaystyle OH}{C}=O$$

Fatty acids travel in the blood in the form of triglycerides. Three fatty acid chains attach to a molecule of glycerol to form a tri (meaning "three") glyceride.

Definitions: Fat and Cholesterol

$$H-\overset{\overset{\displaystyle H}{|}}{\underset{|}{C}}-O-\overset{\overset{\displaystyle H}{|}}{\underset{\underset{\displaystyle H}{|}}{C}}-\overset{\overset{\displaystyle H}{|}}{\underset{\underset{\displaystyle H}{|}}{C}}-\overset{\overset{\displaystyle H}{|}}{\underset{\underset{\displaystyle H}{|}}{C}}-\overset{\overset{\displaystyle H}{|}}{\underset{\underset{\displaystyle H}{|}}{C}}-\overset{\overset{\displaystyle OH}{|}}{C}=O$$

$$H-\overset{\overset{\displaystyle H}{|}}{\underset{|}{C}}-O-\overset{\overset{\displaystyle H}{|}}{\underset{\underset{\displaystyle H}{|}}{C}}-\overset{\overset{\displaystyle H}{|}}{\underset{\underset{\displaystyle H}{|}}{C}}-\overset{\overset{\displaystyle H}{|}}{C}=C-\overset{\overset{\displaystyle OH}{|}}{C}=O$$

$$H-\overset{\overset{\displaystyle H}{|}}{\underset{|}{C}}-O-C=C-\overset{\overset{\displaystyle H}{|}}{\underset{\underset{\displaystyle H}{|}}{C}}-\overset{\overset{\displaystyle H}{|}}{\underset{\underset{\displaystyle H}{|}}{C}}-\overset{\overset{\displaystyle OH}{|}}{C}=O$$

Cholesterol is not a member of the fatty acid family. It has a different chemical structure and is not used for energy.

Healthful, polyunsaturated fats are frequently converted from a liquid to a solid form as with margarine, vegetable shortening, and processed peanut butter. During this hardening process, called hydrogenation, the oils are saturated with hydrogen molecules. Hydrogenated vegetable oils, such as Crisco™, or inexpensive margarines, are equally unhealthful as butter, gravy, and other saturated animal fats. The typical American diet contains too much cholesterol and saturated fat and the typical American is prone to heart disease. Even athletes are not immune! If you exercise for

health and fitness, I recommend that you fuel your body with
healthful foods.

The Vegetarian Athlete

Can a vegetarian athlete get enough protein? Certainly! You
can obtain sufficient protein from grains and vegetables to
develop muscles and maintain strength. If you eat eggs and
dairy products in addition to plant foods you easily meet

your needs. These foods are life-sustaining and highly
nutritious—an egg nourishes a chicken embryo; milk
nourishes a newborn baby. Eggs and milk enhance the
nutritional value of peanut butter, bread, rice, and other
vegetable sources of protein. Athletes who rely on veggies
can easily consume the protein they need. Vegans
(vegetarians who eat only grains, fruits, and vegetables with
no animal products) must combine foods that will form
complete proteins, such as:

chili with corn bread	(beans and grains)
peanuts with mixed nuts	(legumes and seeds)
lentil-rice soup	(legumes and grains)

Diet for a Small Planet by Frances Moore Lappe provides a
step-by-step approach to complementary protein cookery.

Comparing Cheeses

Cheese per 1 oz.	Calories	Protein (gm.)	Fat (gm.)
Blue Cheese	100	6.07	8.15
Brie Cheese	95	5.88	7.85
Camembert	85	5.61	6.88
Cheddar	114	7.06	9.40
Colby	112	6.74	9.10
Cottage, Creamed 4% (1 cup)	217	26.23	9.47
Lowfat 2% (1 cup)	203	31.05	4.36
Lowfat 1% (1 cup)	164	28.00	2.30
Cream	99	2.14	9.89
Edam	101	7.08	7.88
Feta	75	4.03	6.03
Gouda	101	7.07	7.78
Gruyere	117	8.45	9.17
Monterey	106	6.94	8.58
Mozzarella, Whole Milk	80	5.51	6.12
Part Skim	72	6.88	4.51
Muenster	104	6.64	8.52
Neufchatel	74	2.82	6.64
Parmesan, Grated	129	11.78	8.51
Hard	111	10.14	7.32
Port du Salut	100	6.74	8.00
Ricotta, Whole Milk (1 cup)	428	27.70	31.93
Partially Skim (1 cup)	340	28.02	19.46
Romano	110	9.02	7.64
Roquefort	105	6.11	8.69
Swiss	107	8.06	7.78
Pasteurized Process			
American	106	6.28	8.86
Pimiento	106	6.27	8.84
Swiss	95	7.01	7.09
American Cheese Food	93	5.56	6.97
Swiss Cheese Food	92	6.21	6.84
Cold Pack American			
Cheese Food	94	5.57	6.93

Source: Dairy Council Digest.

Cheese per 1 oz.	(mg.) Calcium	(mg.) Cholesterol	(mg.) Sodium
Blue Cheese	150	21	396
Brie Cheese	52	28	178
Camembert	110	20	239
Cheddar	204	30	176
Colby	194	27	171
Cottage, Creamed 4% (1 cup)	126	31	850
Lowfat 2% (1 cup)	155	19	918
Lowfat 1% (1 cup)	138	10	918
Cream	23	31	84
Edam	207	25	274
Feta	140	25	316
Gouda	198	32	232
Gruyere	287	31	95
Monterey	212	N.A.	152
Mozzarella, Whole Milk	147	22	108
Part Skim	183	16	132
Muenster	203	27	178
Neufchatel	21	22	113
Parmesan, Grated	390	22	528
Hard	336	19	454
Port du Salut	184	35	151
Ricotta, Whole Milk (1 cup)	509	124	207
Partially Skim (1 cup)	669	76	307
Romano	302	29	340
Roquefort	188	33	52
Swiss	272	26	74
Pasteurized Process			
American	174	27	406
Pimiento	174	27	405
Swiss	219	24	388
American Cheese Food	163	18	337
Swiss Cheese Food	205	23	440
Cold Pack American			
Cheese Food	141	18	274

Is a vegetarian diet more healthful than eating chunks
of meat? Ideally yes, since meats are filled with heart-
unhealthful cholesterol and saturated fat. I have counselled
several vegetarians who will go to extremes to avoid not only

Foods Rich in Zinc

The best sources of zinc are from foods of
animal origin. The zinc in these foods is better
absorbed than the bound-up zinc from plants.

		mg. zinc
Meats:		
10 avg.	oysters	80.0
3 oz.	liver	5.0
3 oz.	ham	4.0
3 oz.	hamburger	3.8
3 oz.	chicken leg	2.4
7 med.	shrimp	2.0
1 lg.	egg	0.5
Dairy:		
1 oz.	cheese	1.0
1 cup	milk	0.9
Beans:		
1 cup	lentils	2.0
2 tbsp.	peanut butter	1.0
Grains:		
1 oz.	bran flakes	3.7*
¼ cup	wheat germ	3.2
1 cup	oatmeal	1.2
1 sl.	wheat bread	0.5

*Enriched with zinc.   RDA = 15 mg. zinc

Source: J. Pennington and H. Church. *Bowes and Church's Food
Values of Portions Commonly Used.* Harper and Row, Publishers,
N.Y. 1980.

red meat but also white sugar, bleached flour, and processed foods. However, they continue to cook their omeletes in butter and create brown rice casseroles with a rich, sour cream sauce. Many lacto-ovo vegetarians consume lots of cholesterol-laden eggs, smother their pasta with cheeses high in saturated fat, and spread their bread with butter. They forget that fat more than protein is the dietary culprit when it comes to heart disease. If you choose to eat a vegetarian diet for health reasons, I hope that you are consistent and choose healthful foods such as: low-fat milk, cottage cheese, yogurt, part-skim ricotta, farmer's cheese, mozzarella, and soft margarines made from recommended oils, such as corn, sunflower, and safflower.

The vegetarian athlete can easily consume all the protein needed, as well as all of the vitamins and minerals by eating a variety of foods. Sometimes vegetarians don't get enough iron and zinc since these minerals are best found in meats. Iron is important for transporting oxygen; zinc is a part of many of the enzymes that help the body to grow and function properly. Vegetables, dried beans, and grains provide fair amounts of minerals. They also have phytates that interfere with zinc absorption. Their iron is a poorly absorbed form. To alleviate the iron problem I recommend that you include in each meal a food high in vitamin C, such

---

Foods Rich in Vitamin C

These foods supply 100% of the RDA:

6 oz.	orange juice
½ cup	strawberries, frozen
½ medium	cantaloupe
½ medium	green pepper
1 cup	cabbage, raw
1 stalk	broccoli
2 medium	tomatoes
1 large	potato, baked

RDA = 60 mg. vitamin C

---

as juice, potato, broccoli, or tomato.

If you are a meat-eater who wants to turn vegetarian I recommend gradually changing your eating habits to make the transition less dramatic. After his father's heart attack, runner John Lynch decided to give up not just red meats, but also cheese and eggs. He quickly traded in his high-cholesterol-high fat diet for more heart-healthy foods. For years, John's typical dinner had included a half pound of hamburger or steak. This sudden change left him craving for beef. He came to me feeling weak and denied. "It's probably all in my mind, but I don't feel as strong without the meat. Also, I can't seem to satisfy my appetite." I gave him the following suggestions:

1. **Have smaller portions of meat** and larger portions of starches and vegetables.

2. **Make more casseroles with rice or pasta.** Have meatless meals two or three times per week. Steak and burgers will soon feel heavy in your stomach and lose their appeal.

3. **Learn to be a creative cook.** Plan your menu around hearty soups, interesting salads, and meatless concoctions. You'll soon be eating a wider variety of foods—and a wider variety of nutrients.

When I saw John at a road race three months later, he mentioned that he was eating fish and chicken two or three times per week. He'd weaned himself away from red meat. "It slows me down." John was content with his dietary changes.

Chapter 11

Meat-Based Entrees

In the days of the "steak and eggs" training table, meat was an athlete's favorite food: "Eat meat: build muscle." We now recognize that training, rather than diet, builds your muscles, and that carbohydrates, rather than proteins, are heart-healthy choices, and your best muscle fuel.

Meat although not highly recommended today, remains a favorite for many athletes. A heavy meat diet is generally high in cholesterol and saturated fats, two factors associated with heart disease. The following are my tips to help you include meats more healthfully into your diet:

- Eat smaller portions. Your mind may delightfully savor a 12-ounce steak but your body needs only one-third of that amount of protein for the entire day. Most Americans, even at poverty level, eat two to three times the recommended amount of protein.

- Stretch smaller meat portions by cooking Chinese style with lots of vegetables or by making casseroles, soups, and stews. Replace calories from meat with more spaghetti, rice, noodles, potatoes and beans—the carbohydrate foods that are best for your muscles.

- Buy lean meats: expensive hamburger instead of the cheaper, fattier kind; top round instead of chuck steak; pork tenderloin cutlets instead of chops.

- Eliminate extra fats: trim off the visible fat before cooking the steak. Drain the grease before you add the hamburger to the casserole. Skim the fat from the top of the stew. Remove the skin from the chicken before cooking.

- Eat more chicken, fish, turkey, veal, and less beef, pork, lamb, and eggs.

Less expensive meats are as nutritious as the prime cuts. All meat regardless of price is an excellent source of protein, B-vitamins, iron, and zinc. The iron and zinc from meats is absorbed better than that from vegetable or grain sources.

Recipes for Chicken ▶

Chicken Dijon
Orange Chicken with Rice
Lemon Chicken
Chicken Marengo
Maple Chicken
Chicken Parmesan
Chicken with Mushroom Sauce
Sesame Chicken
Chicken Stroganoff
Quick One-Pot Chicken Dinner

See: Homemade Chicken Soup
     Sweet and Sour Fish

Chicken

Chicken meat is a nutritious high protein, low fat food. The skin, however, is loaded with fat, cholesterol, and calories. I remove the skin before I cook it; otherwise I am tempted to eat it.

Chicken meat is a perfect example of muscle physiology. The white and dark meat are two kinds of muscle fibers. The white breast meat is composed primarily of fast-twitch muscle fibers. These are best for bursts of energy, and have a high glycogen content. Gymnasts and basketball players have a high percentage of fast-twitch fibers. The dark meat in the chicken legs and wings is composed primarily of slow-twitch muscle fibers that are best for endurance exercise. Marathoners and long distance bicyclists have a high percentage of slow-twitch fibers. These muscles have a relatively higher fat content. Hence, dark chicken meat has more calories.

> *uncooked white meat — 100 calories per 3½ ounces*
> *dark meat   — 112 calories*

The quickest way to cook chicken is by steaming. When I'm in a ravenous rush, I simply put the chicken in a pan with ½-inch of water, cover, and steam it for 20 minutes. The chicken is moist and tender, as compared to broiling or baking, which dries out the flesh . . . and also requires a lot more gas or electricity.

Chicken Dijon

Delightfully different, and a nice change from the standard sauces. Serve with Orange Rice, and cooked carrots with pineapple.

4 chicken breasts, skinned
1 cup water
2 chicken bouillon cubes
½ cup white wine
2 tbsp. spicy mustard
½ cup yogurt or milk
2 tbsp. flour

Optional: parsley

1. In a large skillet, put chicken, water, bouillon, wine, and mustard.

2. Cover. Bring to a boil; simmer for 20 minutes.

3. Mix flour with yogurt. Stir into sauce.

4. Cover and simmer for 10 minutes.

5. Optional: garnish with parsley.

Yield: 4 servings.

Orange Chicken with Rice

This meal-in-a-pot saves on dishwashing. It goes well with either broccoli or a green salad.

1 chicken, cut up, skin removed
1 large onion, thinly sliced
1½ cups orange juice
3 tbsp. soy sauce
1 cup rice, uncooked

Optional:
1 tsp. curry
¼ tsp. garlic powder
2 green peppers, diced

1. In a large pan, put chicken, onion, orange juice, and seasonings.

2. Cover. Bring to boil, reduce heat; simmer for 10 minutes.

3. Add rice. Cook for 20 minutes, or until rice is done.

4. Optional: arrange green peppers on top. Cover, and cook for 2 to 3 minutes.

Yield: 4 servings.

Lemon Chicken

Serve with rice or Zucchini-Stuffing Casserole.

1 **chicken, cut up**
2 **lemons, thinly sliced**
2 **cups chicken broth, homemade, canned, or from bouillon cubes**
1 **tbsp. oregano**
black pepper

1. Place half the lemon slices in a shallow baking pan.

2. Place chicken on top of the lemon.

3. Pour broth over chicken. Sprinkle with oregano and pepper.

4. Place remaining lemon slices on top of chicken.

5. Bake uncovered at 350°F. for 45 minutes, or until chicken is done.

Yield: 4 servings.

Chicken Marengo

Cook this in a cast-iron skillet to increase the iron content of the sauce. Serve with noodles and a green salad.

1   **chicken, cut up, skin removed**
8   **oz. tomato sauce**
1   **6-oz. can mushrooms**
     or 1 lb. fresh mushrooms, sliced
¾   **cup sherry**
2   **cloves garlic, minced**
pepper
salt

1. Place chicken in a saucepan.

2. Combine remaining ingredients and pour over the chicken.

3. Cover. Bring to boil; simmer for 45 minutes.

4. Skim off fat before serving.

Yield: 4 servings.

Maple Chicken

The maple adds a slightly different flavor. Your guests will wonder what your secret is.

If you prefer to bake the chicken, simply put the ingredients in a covered casserole, and bake at 350°F. for 45 minutes.

Serve this dish with winter squash or green beans.

1   chicken, cut up, skin removed
¼   cup maple syrup
1   tbsp. lemon juice
1½ cups chicken broth, homemade, canned or from
     bouillon cubes
pepper
1   cup rice

Optional: ¼ cup slivered almonds

1. In a large saucepan, put chicken and all the other ingredients except the rice. Cover.

2. Bring to boil; simmer for 10 minutes.

3. Add rice. Cook for 20 minutes, or until rice is done.

4. Optional: garnish with almonds.

Yield: 4 servings.

Chicken Parmesan

For variety, substitute cracker crumbs or crushed cold cereal for the bread crumbs. I usually serve this with baked potatoes and green beans.

1   chicken, quartered, skin removed
¼   cup bread crumbs
¼   cup parmesan cheese
½   cup milk

Optional:
   garlic powder
   oregano
   basil

1.   Mix bread crumbs and parmesan cheese.

2.   Dip chicken pieces in milk, then crumbs. Repeat.

3.   Place in a shallow pan. Bake at 350°F. for 45 minutes.

Yield: 4 servings.

Chicken with Mushroom Sauce

Excellent with rice and spinach salad.

1   chicken, cut up, skin removed
1   can mushroom soup
½   soup-can milk
1   3-oz. can sliced mushrooms
   or ½ lb. fresh mushrooms
½   cup sherry
pepper
salt

1. Place chicken in a casserole dish.

2. Mix the remaining ingredients and pour over chicken.

3. Cover. Bake at 350°F. for 45 minutes.

Yield: 4 servings.

Sesame Chicken

This recipe works well with fish too. Serve with Chinese Rice with Vegetables and Chinese Cucumber Salad.

1	chicken, cut up, skin removed
1	egg
½	cup milk
1	cup flour
1½	tsp. salt
¼	tsp. pepper
¼	cup sesame seeds

Optional:

½	tsp. ginger
½	tsp. garlic salt

1. Preheat oven to 350°F.

2. Beat eggs with milk.

3. In a shallow bowl, mix flour, seasonings, and sesame seeds.

4. Dip chicken in egg, then flour; repeat.

5. Place in baking dish. Bake for 45 minutes.

Yield: 4 servings.

Chicken Stroganoff

Serve over noodles and garnish with parsley.

4 chicken breasts, cut up, skin removed
1 tbsp. oil
1 small onion, diced
2 tsp. lemon juice
1 cup chicken broth, homemade, canned, or from
     bouillon cubes
1 cup yogurt
2 tbsp. flour

Optional:
   pinch thyme
   pinch nutmeg
   ¼ cup sherry

1. In a large skillet, sauté onion in oil until transparent.

2. Add chicken pieces, lemon juice, spices, and broth. Cover, simmer for 20 minutes.

3. Mix flour and yogurt.

4. Stir 2-4 tablespoons hot broth into yogurt. Add back to pan, stirring constantly. Heat gently until thickened.

Yield: 4 servings.

Quick One-Pot Chicken Dinner

When I get home late from work I quickly put this on to cook and it's done by the time I've read the newspaper. For variety, I omit the potato and instead make stuffing by adding the cooking broth to stuffing mix.

chicken pieces, skin removed
potato, ¼-inch slices
pepper
salt

Vegetable of your choice: peas, green beans, zucchini,
   broccoli

1. In a saucepan, with 1 inch water, put sliced potato, chicken, and seasonings.

2. Cover, bring to a boil, and simmer for 20 minutes.

3. Add vegetable. Cook 5 more minutes, or until vegetable is done.

4. Drain and skim the broth. Serve it as a first course to the dinner.

Recipes for Fish and Seafood ▶

Broiled Fish
Baked Fish with Wine
Baked Fish with Cheese
Baked Fish with Lemon
Sweet and Sour Fish
Tuna-Noodle Casserole
Tuna-Broccoli Casserole
Tuna with Green Beans
Tuna-Apple Salad
Tuna Salad in Cantaloupe Halves
Salmon Casserole
Spaghetti with Clam Sauce
Clam Casserole

Fish and Seafood

Fish is a heart-healthy food. Even the fattiest fish is leaner than most meats. Fish fat, which is highly polyunsaturated, is liquid in cold temperatures. If the fish fat were saturated, the fish would be "solid" in the cold ocean, and would be unable to swim.

Some fish do contain more fat—and more calories— than others.

	Calories/ 3½ oz. (raw)		Calories/ 3½ oz. (raw)
oysters	66	halibut	100
sole	68	striped bass	105
lobster	72	bluefish	117
cod	78	perch	118
haddock	79	swordfish	118
scallops	81	tuna	127
clams	82	(water-pack)	
shrimp	91	butterfish	169
crab	93	mackerel	191
pollock	95	rainbow trout	195
		salmon	207

The size and shape of fish influence the cooking time. It is done when the flesh is no longer translucent and flakes easily with a fork.

To remove a fishy odor from your hands, rub them with lemon juice, vinegar, or salt; then wash them.

Broiled Fish

Simple but tasty. Serve with winter squash and garlic spinach.

fish fillets
bottled Italian salad dressing

Optional:
> **oregano**
> **parsley**
> **pepper**
> **salt**

1. Place fish on foil in baking pan.

2. Sprinkle with Italian dressing and seasonings.

3. Broil until fish flakes easily when tested with a fork (about 10 minutes for a ½" thick fillet). Thin fillets cook nicely without being flipped.

Baked Fish with Wine

Vermouth or dry white wine adds a nice flavor to fish. I use leftover wine rather than opening a fresh bottle. Instead of baking this in the oven, you can also simmer it on top of the stove in a skillet. For best results put the vegetables under the fish.

Serve with Rice Parisienne and Colorful Corn.

1½   lb. white fish (scrod, sole, or haddock)
1   large onion, sliced
½   cup vermouth or dry white wine
½   cup milk
1   tbsp. flour
pepper
salt

Optional: sliced mushrooms

1. Place fish in a casserole dish.

2. Add milk, vermouth, onions, and mushrooms.

3. Cover. Bake at 350°F. for 30 minutes.

4. Place fish on a serving platter.

5. Thicken sauce with 1 tablespoon flour that has been mixed with a little cold milk.

6. Stir the flour and milk mixture into the sauce. Bring to a boil.

7. Season with salt and pepper. Pour the sauce over the fish.

Yield: 4 servings.

Baked Fish with Cheese

Simple but delicious. Serve with noodles or rice, and asparagus.

1½ lb. white fish fillets
8   oz. muenster cheese, sliced

Optional:
> sprinkling of paprika or parsley
> salt
> pepper

1. Place fish on greased baking dish. Top with cheese slices.

2. Bake at 425°F. for 15-20 minutes, or until the fish flakes easily when tested with a fork.

Yield: 4 servings.

Baked Fish with Lemon

I serve this with Zucchini-Stuffing Casserole and a green vegetable. When I'm feeling lazy, I omit the chopped onions and celery.

1   lg. onion, chopped
2   stalks celery, chopped
1½ lb. fillets of white fish
¼   cup margarine, melted
2   tbsp. lemon juice
1   tbsp. Worcestershire sauce

Optional:
   sprinkling of parsley
   herbed bread crumbs

1. Preheat oven to 350°F.

2. Place onion and celery on bottom of greased baking dish. Lay fish fillets on top.

3. Mix lemon juice, Worcestershire sauce, and melted margarine. Pour over fish.

4. Bake covered for 20 minutes, or until the fish flakes easily when tested with a fork.

Yield: 4 servings.

Sweet and Sour Fish

This sweet and sour sauce is excellent. I use it with chicken and pork, as well as fish. Serve this dish with rice and green peas.

1½	lb. fish fillets (cod, haddock, or sole)
2	green pepper, cut into strips
1	tbsp. oil
4	tbsp. catsup
3	tbsp. vinegar
3	tbsp. sugar
1	tbsp. cornstarch
¾	cup water

1. Put fish into a greased baking dish. Arrange green pepper strips on top.

2. In a saucepan, combine oil, catsup, vinegar, sugar, and ½ cup water. When boiling, add cornstarch that has been mixed with ¼ cup water. Cook for 1 minute or until thickened.

3. Pour sauce over fish. Bake covered at 350°F. for 30 minutes.

Yield: 2-3 servings.

Tuna-Noodle Casserole

This is a classic casserole that I enjoy better the second day, when the flavors have blended. Serve with carrot and celery sticks.

8   oz. noodles
1   7-oz. can tuna
1   can cream of mushroom soup
½   soup-can milk

Optional:
   peas
   celery
   green pepper
   bean sprouts
   cheese cubes
   grated parmesan
   slivered almonds

Seasonings:
   salt
   pepper
   parsley
   basil
   curry

1.   Cook noodles.

2.   Heat soup, milk, tuna, and seasonings.

3.   Mix with noodles. Add optional ingredients as desired.

4.   This can be served as is if you are in a hurry, or baked for 20 minutes in a 350°F. oven, to allow the flavors to blend.

Yield: 3-4 servings.

Tuna-Broccoli Casserole

This recipe makes a nice change from the traditional tuna-noodle casserole. Serve with Rice Parisienne and Syrian-Bread Mushroom Toasties.

2   pkg. frozen broccoli or 3 stalks fresh broccoli
2   7-oz. cans tuna, drained
1   can cream of mushroom soup
½   soup-can milk
1   cup cheese, cheddar or Swiss, grated

Optional:
   ½   cup bread crumbs or stuffing mix

1. Cook broccoli. Put in shallow baking dish.

2. Add flaked tuna.

3. Mix soup with milk and pour over tuna.

4. Sprinkle cheese on top. Optional: add bread crumbs.

5. Bake at 350°F. for 20 minutes.

Yield: 4 servings.

Tuna with Green Beans

A simple but different way to cook tuna. I bake small potatoes at the same time. The result is a nice hot meal with no dirty dishes! Serve with thick slices of bread, or baked potato.

1   10-oz. pkg. frozen green beans
1   7-oz. can tuna, drained
3   tbsp. Italian dressing
pepper

1.   Place frozen green beans on aluminum foil.

2.   Top with flaked tuna.

3.   Pour salad dressing on top. Sprinkle with pepper.

4.   Seal in foil. Bake at 400°F. for 20–25 minutes.

Yield: 2 servings.

Tuna-Apple Salad

This salad tastes best after it has chilled for an hour. Serve with bread or crackers.

1   can tuna, flaked
½   cup yogurt or mayonnaise
½   tsp. vanilla
½   tsp. curry
¼   cup raisins
2   apples, chopped
¼   cup walnuts, chopped

1.   Mix all the ingredients. Serve on a bed of lettuce.

Yield: 2 servings.

Tuna Salad in Cantaloupe Halves

This makes a cool summertime supper. Cantaloupe is low in calories, high in vitamin C.

1   7-oz. can tuna, flaked
2   stalks celery, sliced
mayonnaise to bind
1   lemon
pepper
salt
1   large cantaloupe

1. Mix tuna, celery, mayonnaise, juice of ½ lemon, salt, and pepper.

2. Cut cantaloupe in half, scoop out the seeds. Sprinkle with remaining lemon juice.

3. Fill with tuna mixture.

Yield: 2 servings.

Salmon Casserole

Prepare this early in the day for that evening's dinner. If you want a slightly richer sauce, use part evaporated milk. Serve with a tossed green salad.

8   oz. noodles
4   tbsp. margarine
4   tbsp. flour
2   cups milk
pepper
salt
1   8-oz. can salmon
1   pkg. frozen peas
1   6-oz. can mushrooms

1. Cook noodles according to directions given on box.

2. In a saucepan, melt the margarine. Stir in the flour. When mixture is thickened, gradually add the milk. Season to taste.

3. Remove from heat. Add noodles, salmon, peas, and mushrooms.

4. Pour into a casserole dish. Bake at 350°F. for 30 minutes.

Yield: 4 servings.

Spaghetti with Clam Sauce

Clams are high in protein, low in calories, cholesterol, and saturated fats. They provide a good source of iron.

½   lb. spaghetti
¼   cup olive oil
2   cloves garlic, minced
1   7-oz. can clams and liquid
cheese, grated
parsley

1. Cook spaghetti according to directions given on the box.

2. Meanwhile, saute garlic in olive oil. Add clams and liquid.

3. Pour over cooked spaghetti. Sprinkle with parsley. Mix well.

4. Serve with grated cheese.

Yield: 3 servings.

Clam Casserole

*The type of cracker influences the taste of this casserole.
Stoned wheat crackers are my preference. To crush them, I
put them in a bag, and pound it with a wine bottle.*

*This is nice as a side dish to a vegetable soup, or as an
entree with a green vegetable and a salad.*

1   7-oz. can clams, minced
2   cups cracker crumbs, unsalted
2   eggs
1   can cream of mushroom soup
1   soup-can milk

1.   Combine all the ingredients in a casserole dish.

2.   Cover. Bake at 350°F. for 45-60 minutes, or until the
center is firm.

Yield: 4 servings.

Recipes for Beef and Pork ▶

Beef:

> **Chili**
> **Sloppy Joes**
> **30-Minute Meat Loaf**
> **Meatza Pie**
> **Goulash**
> **Six-Layer Dinner**

See: Meaty Onion Soup

Pork:

> **Pork Chops with Apples**
> **Sweet and Sour Pork Chops**

Chili

As with most casseroles, the flavor of chili improves with age. I generally make a lot, and enjoy the leftovers at lunch, with cheese and crackers. If you prefer to omit the beef, serve this with rice or corn bread, to enhance the protein value of the beans.

1   **lb. lean hamburger**
1   **large onion, chopped**
2   **1-lb. cans kidney beans**
1   **1-lb. can tomatoes, crushed**
2   **tbsp. chili powder**
pepper
salt

1. In a large skillet, brown the hamburger and onions, and drain the grease.

2. Add the remaining ingredients. Cover. Simmer for ¼ to 2 hours—the longer the better.

Yield: 4 servings.

Sloppy Joes

These make a favorite for a Saturday lunch . . . spicy, and a nice change from a cold sandwich.

By cooking this in a cast-iron skillet, you will get more nutritional value from additional iron in the sauce.

1   lb. hamburger
1   12-oz. bottle chili sauce
hamburger buns or English muffins

Optional: grated cheese

1.   Brown hamburger, drain well.

2.   Add chili sauce and heat.

3.   Serve over English muffins or hamburger buns.

Yield: 4 servings.

30-Minute Meat Loaf

Since this is a cake rather than a loaf, it cooks in 30 minutes. Along with the meat loaf I bake small potatoes or cut large potatoes in half that will cook in the same amount of time.

1	lb. lean hamburger
2	tbsp. dried onion soup mix
½	cup oatmeal
1	egg
1	cup catsup

Optional topping:

¼	cup catsup
1	tbsp. mustard
2	tbsp. brown sugar

1. Mix together all the ingredients.

2. Pat into 9-inch x 9-inch square pan.

3. Bake in 350°F. oven for 30 minutes. Drain grease.

4. Optional topping: Mix together catsup, mustard, and brown sugar. After 20 minutes remove meat loaf from the oven. Drain off the grease. Spread on topping. Bake for 10 more minutes.

Yield: 4-6 servings.

Meatza Pie

I like this recipe because I can mix it in the baking dish. Serve with parmesan or garlic bread, and green beans.

1 lb. lean ground beef
1 tsp. garlic salt
½ cup milk
½ cup fine, dry bread crumbs
1 8-oz. can tomato sauce
1 6-oz. can mushrooms
4 oz. mozzarella cheese, sliced
1 tsp. oregano
2 tbsp. grated parmesan cheese

1. Mix together in a pie pan: beef, garlic salt, milk, and bread crumbs.

2. Spread over the bottom and ½-inch on sides of pan.

3. Spread tomato sauce on top. Add mushrooms.

4. Top with mozzarella slices; sprinkle with seasoning and parmesan cheese.

5. Bake at 400°F. for 30 minutes. Drain the grease. Let stand for a few minutes before cutting in wedges.

Yield: 4-6 servings.

Goulash

The original recipe calls for stew beef but I generally make this with hamburger since it takes less cooking time. Serve with noodles and peas.

1   lb. lean hamburger
1   large onion, chopped
1   clove garlic, crushed
1   8-oz. can tomato sauce
pepper
salt
dash ground cloves
pinch basil
1   tbsp. molasses

1.   In a large skillet, brown hamburger, onion, and garlic. Drain the grease.

2.   Add tomato sauce and seasonings. Cover, simmer for 20 minutes to two hours—the longer, the better the flavor.

Yield: 4 servings.

Six-Layer Dinner

You can cook this dinner in a heavy skillet on top of the stove, or bake it in a casserole. If you don't have all the ingredients simply skip the layer.

1   lb. lean hamburger
4   potatoes, ¼-inch slices
2   large carrots, ¼-inch slices
1   large onion, ¼-inch slices
1   1-lb. can tomatoes, chunked
1   green pepper, ¼-inch slices
pepper
salt

Optional:
    pinch of basil
    sprinkling of garlic powder

1.   Brown the hamburger in a heavy skillet and drain the grease.

2.   Layer the remaining ingredients in the order given.

3.   Cover and simmer for 30 minutes, or bake for 45 minutes at 350°F.

Yield: 4 servings.

Pork Chops with Apples

Great with winter squash.

4   **lean pork chops, trimmed**
1   **onion, chopped**
3   **apples, sliced**
½   **tsp. cinnamon**
pepper
salt

Optional:
   raisins
   celery

1.   Brown pork chops and onion in skillet.

2.   Add 1¼-inch water (or bouillon or cider). Cover and simmer for 20 minutes. Skim the fat.

3.   Add apples. Sprinkle with cinnamon.

4.   Cover, simmer for 15 more minutes.

Yield: 4 servings.

Sweet and Sour Pork Chops

Excellent with Orange Rice and peas.

4   lean pork chops, well trimmed
1   13½-oz. can pineapple chunks with juice
¼   cup molasses
½   cup vinegar
1   tbsp. soy sauce
2   tsp. cornstarch

Optional:
    ½   tsp. ginger
    1   11-oz. can mandarin oranges

1.   Brown pork chops in a large skillet and drain the fat.

2.   Add pineapple juice, molasses, vinegar, soy sauce (and ginger).

3.   Cover; simmer for ½ hour.

4.   Skim the fat.

5.   Combine cornstarch with 1 tablespoon water. Mix into the sauce, stirring constantly, until thick.

6.   Add the fruits and heat.

Yield: 4 servings.

Chapter 12
Meatless Entrees

Recipes with Cheese ▶

Sauteed Onions and Cheese
Spinach Pie
Zucchini-Cheese Casserole
Zucchini "Lasagne"
Spaghetti à la Carbonara
Fettucine
Pizza Strata
"White Rabbit"
French Toasted Cheese Sandwiches
English Muffin Pizzas

See: Baked Noodles with Cheese
Pasta with Broccoli Sauce
Creamed Mushrooms on Toast
Corn and 'Tater Soup

Cheese

Cheese is nutritious, economical, and an important source of calcium, protein, and riboflavin. One pound of cheese contains ten pounds of milk solids. Cheese is also high in saturated fat, sodium and calories so I recommend that you eat it in moderation (2 ounces/day).

- *Cheese tastes best at room temperature. When time permits remove it from the refrigerator one hour before serving it as an appetizer.*
- *Cheese is easiest to shred, grate, or slice when cold. I prefer to grate mozzarella when it is partially frozen.*
- *If mold grows along the edge of the cheese, simply trim off the mold. It will not harm the safety or quality of the remainder. In fact, it adds a nice "blue cheese" flavor.*
- *Grate the odds and ends of old cheese. Add these to casseroles, soups, and hot vegetables. I keep a small bag of grated cheese in my freezer, and simply take a handful when I want a quick garnish for a hot meal.*

Sautéed Onions and Cheese

This was a favorite on my cross-country bicycle trip. Wilf, an Englishman, introduced us to this simple meal. We liked it on mashed potatoes but it also goes well with toast, rice and noodles.

Serve with a colorful vegetable, such as green pepper and tomato salad or peas.

4	large onions, sliced
2-4	tbsp. margarine
pepper	
salt	
4	oz. Swiss or muenster cheese, cubed

1. In a skillet, sauté the onions in margarine until they are very well browned.

2. Arrange the cheese cubes on top of the onions. Let them melt, then stir gently. Season with salt and pepper.

3. Serve on potato, rice, toast, or noodles.

Yield: 2 servings.

Spinach Pie

This dish can be made ahead and baked later. Serve it warm or cold for a meal-on-the-run. I vary it with different vegetables (broccoli, zucchini, or mushrooms) and different herbs (oregano, basil).

Serve with Herbed French Bread and a tossed salad.

1   lb. fresh spinach (or 1 10-oz. frozen pkg.)
1   lb. cottage or ricotta cheese
¼   cup parmesan
¾   cup Swiss, cheddar, or muenster cheese, grated
3   eggs, beaten
1   tsp. salt
½   tsp. pepper
½   tsp. garlic salt

Optional:
  ½   cup mushrooms, sliced
  ¼   cup sunflower seeds

1. Preheat oven to 350°F.

2. In a covered pot with ¼-inch water, steam fresh spinach for 1 minute until limp. Drain; cut into small pieces. (Or cook and drain frozen spinach.)

3. Mix cooked spinach with the remaining ingredients.

4. Pour into greased casserole dish.

5. Bake for 30-40 minutes, or until a knife inserted in the center comes out clean.

Yield: 3 servings.

Zucchini-Cheese Casserole

This recipe is versatile. You can use different types of bread, cheese, and vegetables such as tomato or broccoli instead of zucchini.

8   slices bread, cubed
1   medium zucchini, thinly sliced
      (or other vegetable)
½   lb. Swiss (or other cheese), grated
1½   cups milk
2   eggs, beaten
¾   tsp. salt
½   tsp. dry mustard (optional)
pepper, to taste

1. Preheat oven to 350°F.

2. Arrange bread cubes in a 9-inch pie plate.

3. Top with vegetable and sprinkle with cheese.

4. Beat together eggs, milk, and seasonings.

5. Pour over bread and cheese.

6. Bake for 40 minutes, or until puffy and brown. Serve immediately.

Yield: 4 servings.

Zucchini "Lasagne"

This meal contains fewer calories than a pasta-based lasagne. I vary the recipe by using steamed eggplant instead of zucchini. Serve with hot Parmesan-Garlic Bread and a salad.

1 **medium onion, chopped**
1 **tbsp. oil**
1 **15-oz. can tomato sauce**
½ **tsp. salt**
½ **tsp. oregano**
¼ **tsp. basil**
pepper, to taste
4 **medium zucchini, ¼-inch-thick sliced lengthwise**
½ **lb. cottage cheese**
1 **egg**
2 **tbsp. flour**
½ **lb. mozzarella cheese, grated**

1. Sauté onion in oil until transparent.

2. Add tomato sauce and seasonings; heat to a boil; simmer for 5 minutes.

3. Combine cottage cheese and egg.

4. Arrange half of zucchini in bottom of greased 8-inch x 12-inch baking dish. Sprinkle with 1 tablespoon flour.

5. Top with cottage cheese and half of the tomato sauce.

6. Repeat the layers with the remaining zucchini and flour and tomato sauce. Sprinkle with mozzarella.

7. Bake for 40 minutes at 350°F. until zucchini is fork-tender. Let stand 10 minutes for easier cutting.

Yield: 6 servings.

Spaghetti á la Carbonara

*I frequently serve this as my standard "company-is-coming"
dinner when I have little preparation time. It can be served
either as a main dish with a green vegetable or salad or as a
side dish for a fish meal.*

½	lb. spaghetti
3-6	tbsp. olive oil
1	large onion, chopped (or ¼ tsp. powder)
1	clove garlic, minced
2	tbsp. parsley
1	tsp. oregano
½	cup white wine or vermouth
2	eggs, beaten
6	oz. Swiss or muenster cheese, grated

1. Cook spaghetti. (I add a little oil to the cooking water to
prevent the pasta from sticking.)

2. Meanwhile, in a large saucepan, sauté the onion, garlic,
and spices in oil until tender.

3. Add wine. Add cooked spaghetti. Mix well.

4. Stir in beaten eggs and grated cheese. Let stand for 1-2
minutes to allow the heat of the spaghetti to cook the eggs.

Yield: 4 servings.

Fettucine

Quick and easy! The key is fresh cheese—grate your own. Don't use the pre-grated type. Serve with a green vegetable or tomato and pepper salad.

½   **lb. fettucine, spaghetti or noodles**
2-4 **tbsp. margarine**
½   **lb. fresh parmesan cheese**
pepper
salt

1. Cook pasta; drain.

2. Add margarine and lots of freshly grated parmesan.

3. Season with salt and pepper to taste.

Yield: 2-3 servings.

Pizza Strata

This dish is excellent for a make-ahead meal. Prepare it the night before and refrigerate. Put it in the oven when you get home from work; it will bake while you entertain your guests. Serve with green beans or a salad.

1   medium onion, chopped
1   green pepper, chopped (optional)
1   cup mushrooms, sliced (optional)
2   tbsp. oil
1   6-oz. can tomato paste
2   tsp. oregano
½   tsp. salt
¼   tsp. garlic powder
8   slices bread, crusts removed
2   tbsp. parmesan cheese, grated
8   oz. mozzarella cheese
3   eggs, beaten
2   cups milk

1. Saute vegetables in oil until tender.

2. Add tomato paste and seasonings.

3. Place 4 slices of bread in bottom of buttered 8-inch square baking dish.

4. Spread half of tomato mixture over bread; sprinkle with 1 tablespoon parmesan cheese.

5. Place half of mozzarella over tomato mixture.

6. Repeat bread, tomato, and cheese layers.

7. Combine eggs and milk; pour over bread mixture.

8. Cover; if time permits refrigerate several hours or overnight.

9. Bake at 350°F. for 1 hour, or until knife inserted near center comes out clean.

Yield: 4 servings.

"White Rabbit"

*This quick dinner is tasty served over toast or broccoli. If I
don't have any bread crumbs, I simply substitute 3-4 slices of
crustless bread broken into small pieces.*

1 cup bread crumbs
1 cup milk
1 egg
2 tbsp. margarine
1 cup sharp cheese, grated
½ tsp. salt
½ tsp. dry mustard (optional)
dash cayenne pepper (optional)
crisp toast

1. Combine bread crumbs, milk, egg, and seasonings.

2. In upper part of a double boiler, melt margarine; add
cheese.

3. When cheese is melted, add soaked bread crumb mixture.

4. Cook for 5 more minutes or until thick.

5. Serve over crisp toast or steamed vegetables.

Yield: 4 servings.

French Toasted Cheese Sandwiches

These are quick and easy for brunch as well as for supper. For variety, add sliced ham or sautéed mushrooms to the sandwich filling. Serve with maple syrup and a spinach salad.

2   eggs, beaten
½   cup milk
½   tsp. salt
4   slices bread
cheese, sliced
margarine

Optional:
    sliced ham
    sliced tomato
    sautéed mushrooms
    mustard

1.   Beat eggs, milk, and salt.

2.   Melt margarine in heated skillet.

3.   Dip two slices of bread in egg mixture and place in skillet.

4.   Put cheese slices on bread.

5.   Cover with 2 more slices of bread dipped in egg to complete the sandwich.

6.   Cover the pan. Slowly brown on both sides over low heat until golden.

Yield: 2 sandwiches.

English Muffin Pizzas

I make these by the dozen, wrap them individually, and freeze them. Whenever I need a quick snack or meal I pop a few into the toaster-oven or a covered frying pan.

6   English muffins, split
1   6-oz. can tomato paste or pizza sauce
parmesan cheese
oregano
garlic powder
basil (optional)

Toppings:
    grated cheddar cheese
    mushrooms
    green peppers
    onion
    olives

1. Place English muffin halves on an ungreased baking sheet and spread each half with tomato paste.

2. Sprinkle with parmesan, oregano, basil, and garlic powder.

3. Arrange toppings; sprinkle with cheese.

4. Freeze two hours, or until firm. Wrap individually. Return to freezer.

5. To heat, bake unwrapped at 450°F. for 12 minutes.

Yield: 12 pizzas.

Recipes with Eggs ▶

Stove-Top Broccoli Souffle
Easy Quiche
Egg and Potato Dinner
Tasty Poached Eggs
Cottage Cheese Omelet

See: Egg Drop Soup

Eggs

- *Eggs are a controversial food since they have both good and bad points. On the good side, they are an economical and highly nutritious protein food. They supply all of the essential amino acids, vitamins A, B-complex, zinc, and other nutrients. They keep well in the refrigerator, and are handy for breakfast, lunch, and dinner.*

- *On the negative side, eggs are one of the richest sources of cholesterol. One medium egg contains 265 milligrams of cholesterol, as compared to 30 milligrams in an ounce of cheddar cheese, and 60 milligrams in a small portion of chicken. If you have a family history of heart disease— stroke, heart attacks, high blood pressure—I recommend that you limit your egg intake to three per week. The cholesterol from the egg yolk may contribute to cholesterol build-up in your blood vessels. Enjoy cereal for breakfast and save the eggs for a quick supper.*

- *Although eggs with a white shell are generally more expensive than those with a brown shell, they are nutritionally equivalent.*

- *When you cook eggs, use a low heat. Otherwise the egg white will be tough.*

Stove-Top Broccoli Souffle

This dish doesn't puff like a true souffle—nor does it take as much effort. Serve with fruit salad or green salad and Syrian Bread-Mushroom Toasties.

1	small onion, chopped
1-2	tbsp. oil
1	10-oz. pkg. chopped broccoli (or other fresh or frozen veggie), cooked
6	eggs, beaten
½	cup milk
½	tsp. garlic salt
dash pepper	
½	cup grated parmesan cheese

1. Saute onion in oil in 8-inch heavy skillet.

2. Cover with broccoli.

3. Combine eggs and seasonings.

4. Pour over broccoli, stir once, and sprinkle with cheese.

5. Cover and cook over low heat for 15 minutes, or until a knife inserted in the center comes out clean.

6. Cut into wedges and serve immediately.

Yield: 4 servings.

Easy Quiche

Do you avoid making quiche because of the crust? Crescent roll dough is the easy answer! The vegetables can be sautéed ahead and kept in the refrigerator. Or use leftover, steamed vegetables, or no vegetables. Serve with a salad for dinner. As a snack or appetizer, cut into small pieces.

1	pkg. crescent roll dough
1	medium onion, chopped
1	cup vegetables (mushrooms, zucchini, spinach, broccoli), sliced
1-2	tbsp. margarine
4	eggs
1	cup plain yogurt or milk
1	cup (or more) grated cheese, such as muenster, cheddar

pepper
salt

Optional:
  dash cayenne
  1   tsp. basil
  ½   tsp. curry

1. Preheat oven to 350°F.

2. Unroll crescent roll dough and press into a 9-inch pie pan as crust.

3. Sauté onion in margarine until transparent. Add the other vegetables and sauté until just tender. Arrange on crust.

4. Beat eggs, yogurt, and seasonings. Stir in cheese and vegetables.

5. Pour into crust. Sprinkle with cheese.

6. Bake for 1 hour, or until quiche and crust are golden and a knife inserted into the center comes out clean.

Yield: 3 servings.

Egg and Potato Dinner

This meal is designed for those who hate to wash dishes! It's also good for those who like to exercise after work. Simply put the potato in the oven to bake while you go for an hour's workout.

1   large baking potato
1-2 tsp. margarine
1   egg
1   oz. Swiss cheese, shredded
pepper
salt

1. Pierce a large potato in several places with a fork. Bake in 350°F. oven for one hour, or until done. The potato will be soft. You will be able to pierce it easily with a fork.

2. Make a cross in the top. Fluff up the potato with a fork, and make a "well."

3. Add margarine, if desired, and break the egg into the well. Top with salt, pepper, and cheese. Return to the oven until the egg white is cooked, about 15 minutes.

Yield: 1 serving.

Tasty Poached Eggs

An easy dinner or a pleasant brunch. I enjoy these as a change from plain eggs. Serve with Carrot-Raisin Salad and Glazed Fruit Compote for dessert.

1 tbsp. margarine
1 tbsp. flour
1 cup water
1 tsp. vinegar
½ tsp. salt
1 egg yolk
4 eggs
4 slices toast

1. Melt margarine in 9-inch skillet.

2. Blend in flour. Add water slowly with constant stirring to keep the mixture smooth.

3. Heat to boiling. Stir in salt and vinegar.

4. In a small bowl, beat the egg yolk; add a little bit of hot sauce; beat well. Return this to the hot mixture and stir thoroughly.

5. Have sauce barely simmering and slip eggs one at a time into sauce. (I cook the extra egg white, too.)

6. Cover tightly. Poach 2-3 minutes.

7. Remove lid. Baste eggs with sauce until they are cooked to the desired consistency.

8. Serve on toast with sauce over the top. Garnish with parsley.

Yield: 2 servings.

Cottage Cheese Omelet

Occasionally I'll have an omelet for dinner. I prefer to limit my intake of eggs to 3 per week, since they are high in cholesterol, and heart disease seems to plague my family.

Complete this meal with soup and a salad, or simply toast and tomato juice.

2 eggs
¼ cup milk
pepper
salt
2 tsp. margarine
1 heaping tbsp. cottage cheese

Optional:
    sprinkling of parmesan or cheddar cheese
    strawberry jam
    chopped tomatoes and green peppers

1. Mix egg, milk, and seasonings.

2. Heat margarine in a skillet. Add egg mixture. Tilt pan to distribute egg. With a spatula, lift the side of the omelet to let the uncooked egg flow to the bottom of the pan.

3. When golden on the bottom, spread the cottage cheese and other optional ingredients on the center. Fold the omelet over the cheese and serve.

Yield: 1 serving.

Chapter 13

"V" is for Vegetables, Vitamins, Vim, and Vigor

Vegetables provide a wide variety of vitamins and minerals: A, B-complex, magnesium, and potassium, to name a few. All of which contribute toward helping you to perform at your best. Many vegetables are rich in vitamin C, a vitamin that helps you to maintain strong, healthy tissues, fight infection, and heal cuts. To get the most nutritional value from fresh vegetables, I recommend that you treat them kindly. Otherwise you will reduce some of their nutritional value. Here are my suggestions:

- Wrap leafy vegetables such as lettuce, spinach, and greens in plastic to keep out the air. Oxygen destroys vitamin C.

Save the Vitamin C!

By handling vegetables properly, you can retain more nutritional value. Vitamin C, in particular, is easily destroyed.

Problem	Solution
Air	Wrap produce in plastic. Cook in a covered pan.
Heat	Store produce in the refrigerator. Cook until tender-drisp, not mushy.
Water	Do not soak vegetables in water. Steam in ½-inch of water, or stir fry.
Light	Store produce in dark place. Cook in covered pan.

Although vegetables may lose some of their vitamin C, they will not lose *all* of it.

orange juice,	8 days in refrigerator	= 15% loss
broccoli,	frozen 1 year	= 50%
potato,	stored 8 months	= 40%
tomato,	peeled	= 75%
kale,	stored 2 days, at room temperature	= 40%

Source: R. Harris and E. Karmas, *Nutritional Evaluation of Food Processing.* AVI Publishing Co., Westport, CT., 1975.

- Keep vegetables refrigerated since warmth destroys vitamin C. Asparagus left at room temperature for a day may lose 50% of this nutrient.

- Don't soak vegetables in water. Weight-watcher Joan Caldwell used to refrigerate ready-for-nibbling carrots and celery sticks in a bowl of water. I suggested that she store them in a plastic bag, to retain the water soluble vitamins B and C.

- Eat the peels. Peeling vegetables is a waste of time as well as fiber and nutrients. Vitamin C is stored underneath the skin of many vegetables. If you peel a potato you remove 75% of this nutrient.

Saving the vitamins

Many people think that cooking destroys ALL of the vitamins in vegetables. This is not true. You may lose a percentage of the vitamins that dissolve in water: B-complex, and C, but many others remain. Cooking may actually increase your ability to absorb some of the nutrients, such as vitamin A.

Here are my suggestions for tasty and nutritious vegetables:

Cooking Water is Nutritious

The longer you cook vegetables, the more vitamin C dissolves into the water. Some of the vitamin will be destroyed, but some can be recovered by using the water.

Spinach:	Cooking loss	Recoverable in water	Destroyed
underdone	40%	31%	9%
optimum	55	24	26
overdone	60	12	48

Source: R. Harris and E. Karmas, *Nutritional Evaluation of Food Processing.* AVI Publishing Co., Westport, CT., 1975.

- Cook vegetables quickly, just until they are tender-crisp. The shorter the cooking time, the better their flavor and nutritional value. I steam them in ¼ inch of water in a covered pan, instead of drowning them in 4 inches of water.

- Use the vegetable cooking water for soups and sauces—it is nutritious. I drink it as a broth; the cooking water from peas is my favorite! Spinach may lose 55% of its vitamin C during cooking but you can recover half of this loss in the water.

- Stir-frying vegetables is nutritionally superior to boiling or steaming since the water-soluble vitamins will not be lost. I use a heavy frying pan; it works as well as a Chinese wok. I simply heat the pan, add a little oil, toss in the chopped veggies, and stir them as they cook over high heat.

- For variety, sprinkle in a few herbs while the veggies cook: oregano with zucchini, ginger with carrots, mint with peas.

- Cook acid foods, such as tomatoes, in a cast-iron pot—it is a great source of iron. Spaghetti sauce that has simmered for three hours in an iron pot increases in iron content from 3 to 88 milligrams per one-half cup servings. The natural iron in vegetables is poorly absorbed by the body. You're better off cooking in cast-iron pans than selecting iron-rich veggies, such as spinach and broccoli.

Most veggies are healthful, low-calorie munchies unless you add a lot of fattening butter, cheese sauce, or soured cream. Some vegetables do, however, have significant amounts of calories. If you are watching your weight I recommend that you eat beets, peas, corn, winter squash, and carrots in moderation. If you don't like vegetables or find that they spoil before you get around to eating them, try drinking tomato juice or V-8™ juice. Eat pizza or pasta with tomato sauce. Heat up some vegetable soup. With these ideas you'll survive in good health.

Fresh, Frozen, or Canned?

I am frequently asked, "Are fresh vegetables better than frozen or canned ones?" People are surprised when I tell them frozen and canned veggies do have nutritional value. In fact, they may be better than "fresh" from California, if you live in New England. By the time the vegetables are picked, packaged, shipped to the warehouse, sent to the local market, sit in your car all afternoon, get shoved to the back of the refrigerator, and then finally are eaten a few days later, they are no longer fresh. Even with refrigeration spinach loses half of its vitamin C in five days.

Frozen vegetables are a good choice especially if you live alone and the big bunch of broccoli lasts for the whole week. Freezing retains most nutrients except for vitamin E. (Vegetables contain very little vitamin E so this is an insignificant loss.) If frozen broccoli were to stay in your freezer for six months it might lose 50% of its vitamin C. Since most people don't store food that long, this is not a common problem. Canned vegetables are nutritionally similar to frozen ones. The commercial canning process cooks the veggies much more efficiently than home methods and retains approximately 80% of all the nutrients. When heating canned vegetables, don't overcook them. Simply warm them in the water in which they are packed.

Fiber in Vegetables

In the Salad chapter I mentioned that lettuce is a low-fiber food. Are you wondering which vegetables do supply fiber? Veggies with edible seeds (tomatoes, cucumbers) and skins (potatoes, eggplant) are highest in fiber. Cooking does not significantly reduce the fiber content.

To meet the daily recommended 5–6 grams of fiber I recommend that you choose from the following:

	gm. fiber/½ cup
winter squash	1.6
peas	1.6
lima beans	1.4
broccoli	1.1
eggplant	.9
carrots	.8
cole slaw	.8
corn	.7
baked potato	.7

Getting sufficient fiber from vegetables may be difficult. Grain foods—such as bran flakes or brown rice—are the primary source.

Rules for Cooking Vegetables

1. Wash vegetables thoroughly to remove soil and traces of spray.

2. Put ¼-inch water in the bottom of the pan.

3. Bring water to a boil; add vegetable.

4. Cover pan tightly and cook over medium-low heat until vegetables are tender-crisp.

5. Drain vegetables, reserving cooking liquid for soup or sauces.

Timetable for Steaming Vegetables[1]

Vegetable	Minutes	Vegetable	Minutes
asparagus, whole	10-20	kale	10-15
asparagus tips	5-15	onions, small whole	15-30
beans, whole string	15-30	parsnips, quartered	8-15
beans, frenched string	12-20	peas	8-15
beets	30-45	potatoes, quartered	
beet greens	5-15	sweet	15-20
broccoli	15-20	potatoes, quartered	
carrots, sliced	10-20	white	10-15
cauliflower, whole	15-20	spinach	3-10
cauliflower flowerets	8-15	squash, winter,	
collards	10-20	2-inch pieces	15-20
eggplant, diced	10-15	squash, sliced summer	5-12

*As vegetables differ in texture according to maturity, directions for cooking time can only be approximate.

[1] Source: Heslin, Jo-Ann. *No-Nonsense Nutrition*, CBI Publishing Co., Inc. Boston MA, 1978.

Recipes for Vegetables ▶

Green Beans with Mushrooms
Cooked Carrots with Pineapple
Cooked Cole Slaw
Colorful Corn
Eggplant Parmesan
Summer Vegetable Stew
Spinach with Garlic
Zucchini Italiano
Sautéed Mushrooms
Creamed Mushrooms on Toast
Onion Casserole
Squash with Walnuts and Applesauce

Green Beans with Mushrooms

Green beans are low in calories (30 per cup) as well as nutritional value. Unlike the darkest vegetables such as spinach and broccoli, green beans have marginal amounts of vitamins A and C.

1   medium onion, finely chopped
½   lb. fresh mushrooms, sliced, or
   1 6-oz. can mushrooms
2   tbsp. oil
½   lb. fresh green beans, cut up, or 1 pkg. frozen
pepper
salt

1.   Sauté onion and mushrooms in oil.

2.   Add cut up green beans and ¼ cup water.

3.   Cover and cook for 10-15 minutes or until beans are tender.

Yield: 3 servings.

Cooked Carrots and Pineapple

Carrots are an excellent source of vitamin A. One five-inch carrot will meet 100% of your need for the day.
   This dish is a nice accompaniment for chicken and rice.

4   **large carrots**
1   **1-lb. can pineapple chunks**
½   **tsp. salt**
1   **tsp. cornstarch**
Optional: 1 tbsp. margarine

1.   Thinly slice carrots on the diagonal.

2.   Drain pineapple juice into a saucepan. Reserve 2 tablespoons of juice.

3.   Add carrots and salt. Cover. Cook 8-10 minutes until tender-crisp.

4.   Add pineapple chunks.

5.   Mix cornstarch with reserved juice. Stir into carrot mixture. Cook until thickened.

Yield: 4 servings.

Cooked Cole Slaw

This is a variation on cole slaw. In the wintertime, I prefer warm foods . . . and this is my "hot salad."
   Cabbage is a good source of vitamin C. Cooking will destroy some of the vitamin C content, but will not destroy all of it.

2   tbsp. margarine
3   cups cabbage, shredded
1   large carrot, grated
¼   cup vinegar
2   tbsp. sugar
pepper
salt

1. Melt margarine in a large skillet. Add remaining ingredients.

2. Cover, cook over medium heat for 8 minutes. Stir occasionally.

Yield: 4-6 servings.

Colorful Corn

I prefer to use frozen rather than canned corn because it has less sodium:

	sodium/½ cup
Fresh corn:	*trace amount*
½ cup frozen:	*trace amount*
½ cup canned:	*200 mg.*

1   10-oz. box frozen corn, or 1 1-lb. can corn
1   green pepper, chopped
1   small onion, chopped
1   tomato, seeded and chopped
1   tbsp. oil

1. Sauté pepper and onion in oil until tender.

2. Add corn and tomato. Cover. Cook until heated.

Yield: 3-4 servings.

Eggplant Parmesan

I steam the eggplant, instead of frying it. This saves on time as well as on empty fat calories. For a low-calorie meal, serve this with a salad and toasted Syrian bread. For more substance, serve with pasta.

Eggplant is a high fiber, low-calorie vegetable. It is mostly water, and has insignificant amounts of nutrients.

1 large eggplant
1 28-oz. can tomato puree
1 tbsp. oregano
1 clove garlic, crushed or ¼ tsp. garlic powder
1 tbsp. molasses
1 lb. low-fat cottage cheese
¼ tsp. garlic powder
1 tsp. oregano
2 tbsp. flour
4 oz. low-fat mozzarella
2 tbsp. parmesan cheese

1. Slice eggplant into ½-inch wheels. Steam in ½-inch of water for 10 minutes.

2. Meanwhile, heat tomato puree with 1 tablespoon oregano, garlic, and molasses.

3. Mix cottage cheese with 1 teaspoon oregano, ¼ teaspoon garlic powder, and 2 tablespoons flour.

4. In a casserole, put layer of eggplant, then cottage cheese, then tomato sauce. Repeat layers.

5. Top with grated mozzarella and parmesan.

6. Bake at 350° F. uncovered, for 20 minutes.

Yield: 4 servings.

Summer Vegetable Stew

When your vegetable garden starts to overflow this stew will help you enjoy the bounty. It also freezes very nicely.

This is a nice accompaniment to Easy Quiche or Fettucini.

1	tbsp. oil
1	large onion, chopped
1	clove garlic, crushed
1	medium eggplant, cubed
1	large zucchini, cubed
6	tomatoes, cut up or 1 28-oz. can tomatoes
1-2	tbsp. sugar or molasses
½	tsp. basil
pepper	
salt	
½	cup cheddar or swiss cheese, grated

Optional:

1	bay leaf
1	tbsp. parsley

1. In a large pot, sauté the onion in oil.

2. Add the remaining ingredients except cheese. Cover, cook for 20 minutes, or until tender.

3. Put into shallow baking dish. Sprinkle with cheese. Optional: brown under the broiler before serving.

Yield: 6 servings.

Spinach with Garlic

Spinach, like all dark green vegetables, is rich in vitamin A. One-third cup provides 100% of your daily need. Spinach is also a good source of folic acid, vitamin C, riboflavin, and many other nutrients. By cooking it in oil, rather than water, it will retain more nutritional value.

1   lb. fresh spinach
2   tbsp. oil
1   clove garlic, crushed, or ¼ tsp. garlic powder

1.   Wash spinach; remove tough stems. Drain well.

2.   Heat oil in skillet, add garlic.

3.   Add spinach, stir. Cook, covered for 1 minute over moderately high heat. Uncover; stir gently for 1-2 more minutes.

Yield: 4 servings.

Zucchini Italiano

Zucchini and summer squash are watery vegetables with insignificant nutritional value other than some fiber. They are low in calories . . . until you add oil and cheese!

2   zucchini
4   tbsp. olive oil
parmesan cheese

Optional: parsley flakes

1.   Slice zucchini *very* thinly.

2. In hot olive oil, sauté zucchini slices until browned.

3. Drain on paper towel. Put in oven to keep warm until all zucchini is cooked.

4. Sprinkle liberally with parmesan cheese. Garnish with parsley flakes.

Yield: 4 servings.

Sautéed Mushrooms

Yummy! Mushrooms are low-calorie (until you smother them with cheese). They have an insignificant amount of nutrients.

These are a tempting appetizer or an elegant accompaniment to a meal.

12   oz. fresh mushrooms
2   tbsp. margarine
½   cup white wine
salt
pepper

½   cup parmesan cheese

1. Remove stems from mushrooms. I save the stems, and add them to soups or rice.

2. In a skillet, melt the margarine. Add the mushroom caps and wine, salt, and pepper.

3. Cover. Cook over moderate heat for 5–10 minutes.

4. Uncover. Let the juice evaporate.

5. Sprinkle with parmesan cheese.

Yield: 4 servings.

Creamed Mushrooms on Toast

This dish nicely accompanies chicken and fish, or it can be a substantial entree by itself. For extra flavor, I sometimes add sherry to the sauce.

12   oz. fresh mushrooms, sliced
2   large onions, sliced
2   tbsp. margarine
2   tbsp. flour
1   cup milk
pepper
salt

toast
grated cheese

1. Sauté mushrooms and onions in margarine.

2. Stir in 2 tablespoons flour, making a paste.

3. Slowly add milk, stirring constantly. Season.

4. Serve on toast and sprinkle with grated cheese.

Yield: 4 servings.

Onion Casserole

As with most casseroles, this improves with age. It tastes best when made ahead and reheated.

I enjoy this as a change from the "same ol' vegetables." Since it is high in sodium, I serve it with low-sodium chicken and fish dishes, and winter squash for color. Onions have a lot of flavor, but insignificant nutritional value.

2   16 oz. jars boiled onions, drained
1   8-oz. can mushrooms, drained or 12-oz. fresh
1   can cream of celery soup
½   cup dry vermouth
½   cup parmesan cheese, grated

Optional:
   cracker crumbs or stuffing mix
   parsley

1.   In a casserole dish, mix soup, vermouth, and cheese.

2.   Add onions and mushrooms.

3.   Optional: top with cracker crumbs or stuffing mix. Garnish with parsley.

4.   Bake at 350°F. for 30 minutes. (If you are in a rush, you can simmer this on top of the stove for 15 minutes rather than heating it in the oven.)

Yield: 4-6 servings.

Squash with Walnuts and Applesauce

Winter squash, like most colorful vegetables, is rich in vitamin A. One ¾ cup serving supplies 100% of your daily need. Squash is also a good source of potassium, fiber, and carbohydrates. I recommend it as a part of your pre-competition carbohydrate-loading dinner.

2	acorn squash
1	cup applesauce
2	tbsp. brown sugar
2	tbsp. raisins
2	tbsp. walnuts
¼	tsp. cinnamon

1. Cut squash in half. Scoop out the seeds.

2. Mix together the remaining ingredients.

3. Portion into each half of the squash.

4. Bake covered with ½-inch of water in bottom of pan, in 350°F. oven for ½ hour. Uncover and bake an additional ½ hour or until tender when pierced with a fork.

Yield: 4 servings.

Recipes for Side Dishes ▶

Baked Noodles with Cheese
Pasta with Broccoli Sauce
Spinach Stuffing
Zucchini Stuffing Casserole
Rice Parisienne
Orange Rice
Chinese Rice with Vegetables
Burgundy Beans

Side Dishes

"How much should I cook?" is my standard dilemma when it comes to rice, noodles, and spaghetti. I have trouble remembering how much these foods expand. These guidelines are helpful:

	Raw	*Cooked*	*Calories*
Spaghetti	*8 oz.*	*4 cups*	*800*
Noodles	*8 oz.*	*4 cups*	*800*
Rice	*1 cup*	*3½ cups*	*700*

These amounts will serve four normal appetites. If you are carbohydrate-loading, you should consider eating the whole 1-pound box of pasta!

When I cook pasta, I add a tablespoon or so of oil to the water. This prevents the strands from clumping together once they are cooked and drained.

I usually cook extra pasta and rice and store it in the refrigerator in a covered container. Cooked pasta can be converted into an easy dinner the next night. I heat it in boiling water, drain, and then add a generous amount of grated cheese and a sprinkling of garlic powder and oregano. Or, I mix it with browned hamburger and green peppers, scramble it with eggs, add it to soup, or mix it with kidney beans. Leftover pasta and rice are handy bases for a quick meal.

Baked Noodles with Cheese

When I'm in a hurry, I substitute 2 tablespoons of dried onion soup for the onion, and I heat the casserole on the stove-top instead of in the oven. The original recipe calls for soured cream, but I instead use evaporated milk, a more healthful choice. Serve with Tomato-Pepper Salad.

8   oz. fine noodles
2   cups cottage cheese
1   13-oz. can evaporated milk
¼   tsp. garlic powder
1   onion, finely chopped
2   tbsp. Worcestershire sauce
salt
dash of Tabasco sauce

Optional:
   dill
   celery seed
   parmesan cheese on top

1. Cook noodles; drain.

2. Combine remaining ingredients. Add to noodles.

3. Pour into greased casserole dish, cover.

4. Bake in 350°F. oven for 30 minutes.

Pasta with Broccoli Sauce

Broccoli is an excellent source of vitamin C. One stalk provides 100% of the RDA. Serve with baked fish and sliced tomatoes.

1   bunch fresh broccoli, chopped
     or 2 pkg. frozen broccoli, chopped
¼ cup olive oil
2   (or more) garlic cloves, minced
8   oz. thin spaghetti, cooked
1   cup parmesan cheese
salt
pepper

1. Sauté garlic in olive oil for 3 minutes.

2. Add broccoli. Cover; cook, stirring occasionally, until sauce-like consistency (about 20 minutes—add water as needed).

3. Pour sauce over cooked pasta.

4. Sprinkle generously with cheese.

Yield: 4 servings.

Spinach Stuffing

This looks pretty, and tastes good as well. To convert it into a main dish, I add 2 cans of tuna.
This goes well with fish, chicken, and egg dishes.

9	oz. frozen spinach, chopped
2	cups seasoned stuffing mix
½	cup parmesan cheese, grated
1	large onion, finely chopped
2	eggs, beaten
2-4	tbsp. margarine, melted
1	cup milk
½	tsp. garlic salt

Optional:

½ cup chopped walnuts
2 cans tuna

1. Cook spinach in ½ cup water.

2. Combine with remaining ingredients.

3. Spread in greased casserole dish. Cover.

4. Bake in 350°F. oven for 30 minutes.

Yield: 4-6 servings.

Zucchini Stuffing Casserole

This side dish provides a nice change of pace served with chicken or fish. For extra color cook a grated carrot along with the zucchini.

3   medium zucchini, sliced
1   onion, sliced
½   cup water
1   can cream of chicken (or mushroom) soup
1   soup can milk
3   cups stuffing mix
1/3   cup cheese, grated

1. Put zucchini, onions, and water in a saucepan. Cover. Bring to boil; simmer for 5 minutes.

2. Add soup and milk. Heat.

3. Meanwhile, place stuffing in bottom of a shallow casserole dish.

4. Pour over zucchini mixture.

5. Top with cheese.

6. Cover. Bake at 350°F. for 20 minutes.

Yield: 6 servings.

Rice Parisienne

Try this when you're tired of plain ol' rice.

¼ cup margarine
1 cup rice
½ pkg. onion soup mix
1¾ cups water
1 6-oz. can mushrooms, or
    ½ lb. fresh mushrooms, sliced

Optional: ¼ cup sherry

1. Heat to a boil the water, soup mix, margarine, and mushrooms.

2. Add rice. Cover and simmer for 20 minutes.

Yield: 3–4 servings.

Orange Rice

This rice goes well with chicken or fish.

½ cup orange juice
2 cups water
3 chicken bouillon cubes
2-4 tbsp. margarine
1 cup rice, uncooked

1. Bring water, juice, bouillon, and margarine to a boil.

2. Add rice, stir. Cover and cook over low heat for 20 minutes or until tender.

Yield: 4 servings.

Chinese Rice with Vegetables

A colorful side dish especially when served with chicken and fish.

2½   cups water
2   tbsp. soy sauce
2-4 tbsp. oil
1   cup rice

2 cups vegetables, chopped, your choice of:
    broccoli
    green beans
    Chinese cabbage
    peas
    mixed vegetables
    carrots
    mushrooms
    peppers

1. Bring water, soy sauce, and oil to a boil.

2. Add rice, stir. Cover and cook over low heat for 15 minutes.

3. Add chopped vegetables.

4. Cover, cook for 5 more minutes or until rice and vegetables are done.

Yield: 4 servings.

Burgundy Beans

This dish can either be an accompaniment or an entree. To enhance the protein value, serve it with Crunchy Corn Bread.

1 tbsp. oil
1 onion, chopped
1 green pepper, chopped
1 clove garlic, minced, or ¼ tsp. garlic powder

Optional: 4 slices bacon, fried and crumbled

1 tsp. dry mustard, or 2 tsp. prepared mustard
1 tbsp. brown sugar
1 cup red wine
1 8-oz. can tomato sauce
2 27-oz. cans kidney beans, drained
pepper
salt

1. Saute vegetables in oil until tender.

2. Combine with remaining ingredients in baking dish.

3. Bake at 350°F. for 45–60 minutes, or cook in a saucepan over low heat for 20 minutes.

Yield: 6–8 servings.

Chapter 14

Sugar, Sweets, and Other Treats

Being a nutritionist has its frustrations. For example, my sweet-toothed colleagues hide from me when they eat their desserts. My secretary gobbles her candy bar at the vending machine. She's afraid that I might scold her if I saw her eating it in the office. Most nutritionists realize that sweets—in moderation—can fit into your diet. They can even contribute vitamins and minerals if you make wise choices, such as carrot cake, date squares, and baked apples.

Keep in mind that the fundamental 1500 calories from a

variety of wholesome foods can supply you with the recommended daily allowance for the nutrients you need for health. People who exercise rigorously (more than one hour each day) require more than twice this amount of calories. Although I recommend that you get the extra calories in breads, muffins, noodles, fruit, juice, and vegetables, you do have space for a few sweets. The "junk food junkie" can survive without malnutrition. Your teeth might fall out—sugar does contribute to dental decay—but your muscles will still function. When candy bars and cookies replace your meals nutrition problems are more likely to occur. Eating a lot of sugar contributes directly to dental cavities, but only indirectly to other diseases. Too many desserts, goodies, and sweets may lead to obesity. This, in turn, can result in heart disease, diabetes, hypertension, or other health problems.

In September of 1979 I counselled an Olympic hopeful who was training for the crew team. He was doing everything he could to improve his performance: yoga for flexibility, ballet for balance, nautilus for strength, but he claimed, "My diet is awful." Jim admitted to eating a doughnut each morning during his break time. He assumed that this one "sin" would negate all the nutritional value of his daily yogurt, wheat germ, brewer's yeast, fresh fruits, and other wholesome foods. I assured him that sugar did not

Burning Off The Calories

These figures are based on a 150-pound person. Lighter-weight people burn fewer calories per minute.

Food	Calories	Minutes of Activity Time		
		Walking 3½ mph	Cycling 10 mph	Running 8 mph
orange juice, 8 oz.	110	20	16	7
honey dip donut	260	47	37	17
Oreos™, 4	200	36	29	13
ice cream, ¼ cup	200	36	29	13
cheese pizza, ¼ of 14-inch	350	64	50	23
beer, 12 oz.	150	27	24	10

have negative value. His one honey dip doughnut would not cause his well-balanced diet to deteriorate into a nutritional disaster. He was eating 5,000 calories daily, and getting more than adequate amounts of nutrients in that huge quantity of food.

Some desserts do have a lot of calories. If you train on the theory: "The more I exercise, the more I can eat," you probably work off your daily dessert. However, some athletes tend to overcompensate. Keep in mind that the 150-pound runner burns only 100 calories per mile. Did he run the full six miles to work off that apple pie with ice cream?

Honey vs. Sugar

Many athletes avoid white sugar but use other sweeteners. They do not understand that sugar in any form—honey, brown sugar, raw sugar, maple syrup, or jelly—has insignificant amounts of vitamins and minerals. You would have to eat 200 tablespoons of honey to meet the RDA for calcium, 55 tablespoons of brown sugar to meet the RDA for iron. If you spend your precious money on honey thinking that it is nutritionally superior to sugar you are wasting your pennies. White sugar and honey are biochemically similar: both break down into glucose and fructose. Fructose is then converted into glucose in the liver before it is used by the muscles.

Honey	vs.	Sugar
38% fructose		50% fructose
31% glucose		50% glucose
10% other sugars		
17% water		
4% undetermined		

Some of my patients feel guilty because candy is a psychologically important part of their diet. They want to eat less candy but are afraid of "withdrawal pains." If you would like to curb your sweet tooth I suggest that you start by gradually reducing your sugar intake. Going "cold turkey" may be unrealistic. Ration yourself to only one oatmeal raisin cookie per day or three—rather than seven—ice cream

Nutritional Value of Sugar

	Calories per tbsp.	Calcium mg.	Iron mg.	Riboflavin mg.
White	46	Trace	—	—
Brown	52	11	.4	—
Honey	64	4	.2	.014
R.D.A.		800	18	1.8

J. Pennington and H. Church, *Bowes and Church's Food Values of Portions Commonly Used.* Harper and Row, Publishers, N.Y. 1980.

cones per week. Treat yourself instead to high quality fruits and vegetables that normally you don't buy.

If you plan to eat cookies, candy, and pastry, at least choose ones that have been made from wholesome foods. The following suggestions are a little better than pure sugar:

Sweets with some nutritional value:

oatmeal-raisin cookies	maple walnut ice cream
date bars	banana split with nuts
carrot cake	chocolate covered peanuts
cheese Danish	peanut brittle
pumpkin pie	popcorn balls
apple crisp	sesame candy

Recipes for Desserts ▶

Apple-Bread Pudding
Blueberry Slump
Orange-Pineapple Dessert
Pumpkin Custard
Rum Raisin Ice Cream
Plum Cake
Date Bars
Sautéed Bananas and Oranges
Strawberry-Lemon Yogurt
Yogurt Topping for Fruit
Crisp and Chewies
Maple-Oat Crunchies
Ricotta Delight
Choco-Butter Graham Crackers
Ricotta Pound Cake

*See: Fruit Salad
        Blueberry Muffins*

Apple-Bread Pudding

This dessert is not only nutritious, but also doubles as an excellent breakfast! I enjoy the leftovers for next morning's special treat. Different types of breads vary the flavor. Cracked wheat is my favorite. Serve plain, with yogurt topping, or with ice cream.

4	apples, chopped
6	slices bread, cubed
3	cups milk
3	eggs
½	cup sugar
½	tsp. salt
2	tsp. cinnamon

Topping:

2	tbsp. sugar
1	tsp. cinnamon

1. Put bread cubes and chopped apples into a greased baking dish.

2. In a separate bowl, combine milk, eggs, sugar, salt, and cinnamon.

3. Pour over the apples and bread.

4. Top with 2 tablespoons sugar mixed with 1 teaspoon cinnamon.

5. Cover. Bake at 325°F. for 45 minutes or until set. Pudding is done when a knife inserted near the center comes out clean.

Yield: 6 servings.

Blueberry Slump

Great for carbohydrate-loading!

1   qt. blueberries, fresh or frozen
½   cup water
½   cup sugar

Dumplings:
   1   cup flour
   ½   tsp. salt
   2   tbsp. sugar
   2   tsp. baking powder
   1/3   cup milk
   2   tbsp. oil

1. In a 2-quart saucepan, bring to a boil the blueberries, water, and sugar.

2. Lightly mix together all dumpling ingredients.

3. Drop dumpling dough by spoonfuls into the boiling blueberries.

4. Cover and cook for 20 minutes over moderate heat.

Yield: 4 servings.

Orange-Pineapple Dessert

Easy! . . . And it makes no dishes to wash, except for the one you bake it in. You can easily vary the recipe by using different fruits and cake mixes, and by sprinkling juice instead of margarine on top.

This dessert is rich enough as is. But, if you want more calories, ice cream goes nicely.

1   20-oz. can crushed pineapple
8   oz. orange juice
1   box yellow cake mix (2-layer size, without
      pudding added)
1   stick margarine
1   cup nuts, chopped

1. Preheat oven to 350°F.

2. In a 9-inch x 13-inch pan, mix pineapple and orange juice.

3. Sprinkle all over with dry cake mix. Pat down with spoon.

4. Dot with 1 stick margarine, cut up. Sprinkle with nuts.

5. Bake for 1 hour.

Yield: 12 servings.

Pumpkin Custard

Pumpkin pie without the crust makes an easy dessert with fewer calories and less work!

1   1-lb. can pumpkin
1   13-oz. can evaporated milk
1   tsp. salt
2   eggs
¾   cup brown sugar
1   tsp. cinnamon
½   tsp. ginger
½   tsp. nutmeg
½   tsp. cloves

1.   Preheat oven to 425°F.

2.   Combine all ingredients and pour into a greased casserole dish.

3.   Bake for 45-55 minutes or until a knife inserted near the center comes out clean.

Yield: 6 servings.

Rum Raisin Ice Cream

By softening ice cream and mixing in the ingredients of your choice you can create many delicious concoctions. Banana rum is another favorite.

Ice cream seems to be a favorite food of many athletes. It does have nutritional value since it is made from milk. It is, however, high in saturated fat. Ice milk is a better choice. Ice milk also has more carbohydrates and is better for making glycogen.

1   qt. vanilla ice cream, softened
½   cup raisins
½   cup rum
½   cup nuts, chopped

1.   Soften the ice cream by letting it stand for 30-60 minutes in the refrigerator.

2.   Meanwhile, soak the raisins in the rum.

3.   Mix together the ice cream, raisins, rum, and nuts in a large bowl.

4.   Put into a container and refreeze.

Plum Cake

This easy-to-make cake always comes out perfect, with a gentle, spicy taste. For extra "spice," lace it with a little brandy. Or, for variety, use different fruits, such as apricots or applesauce.

2	eggs
1	cup oil
1-1½	cups sugar
2	cups flour
2	3½-oz. jars baby-food plums
1	tsp. salt
1	tsp. cinnamon
1	tsp. cloves
1	tsp. baking soda
1	tsp. baking powder

Optional:

    ½ cup chopped nuts
        raisins

1. Preheat oven to 375°F.

2. Mix all ingredients; beat well.

3. Pour into a greased tube pan or a 9-inch x 12-inch pan.

4. Bake for 70 minutes for tube pan; or 45 minutes for 9-inch x 12-inch oblong pan; or until toothpick inserted near center comes out clean.

Yield: 12–16 servings.

Date Bars

Perfect for carbohydrate-loading!

¼	cup margarine
8	oz. chopped dates
½-1	cup sugar
2	eggs
½	tsp. salt
¼	tsp. baking powder
½	cup flour

Optional:
   1 cup walnuts, chopped
   ½ tsp. cinnamon

1. Preheat oven to 350°F.

2. In a saucepan, melt margarine.

3. Remove from the heat and add the dates, eggs, sugar, and salt. Beat well.

4. Mix in the baking powder, and then gently stir in the flour.

5. Pour into an oiled 9-inch x 9-inch pan. Bake for 45 minutes, or until a toothpick inserted near the center comes out clean.

Yield: 12 servings.

Sautéed Bananas and Oranges

This dessert looks tempting, tastes good, and is nutritious. Stir it carefully to maintain its attractiveness. Great for breakfast as well as dessert.

Bananas and oranges are rich in potassium and vitamin C.

4   large bananas, cut in 2-inch chunks
2   medium oranges, peeled and sliced
¼   cup brown sugar
4   tbsp. margarine
½   tsp. cinnamon

Optional:
    raisins
    walnuts
    sliced apple

1. In a heavy skillet, melt margarine, brown sugar, and cinnamon over low heat.

2. Add bananas and oranges. Cover; stirring occasionally. Cook 5 minutes or until fruit is heated through.

Yield: 4-6 servings.

Strawberry-Lemon Yogurt

A colorfully appealing and nutritious dessert. The strawberries are a good source of vitamin C; the yogurt supplies calcium and protein.

1   cup lemon yogurt
1   cup strawberries, sliced
¼   cup almonds, toasted

1.   Mix yogurt and strawberries.

2.   Put in serving dish and garnish with almonds.

Yield: 2 servings.

Yogurt Topping for Fruit

I especially enjoy this on fresh berries.

2-4   tbsp. brown sugar
dash salt
2   cups plain yogurt
¾   cup cream, whipped

1.   Combine sugar, salt, and yogurt.

2.   Fold in whipped cream.

3.   Serve over fresh or canned fruit.

Yield: 8 servings.

Crisp and Chewies

As the name suggests these cookies are crisp, yet chewy—a childhood favorite that goes nicely with a glass of milk.

¾	cup margarine
1	egg
¼	cup molasses
1	cup sugar
½	tsp. ginger
½	tsp. cloves
½	tsp. salt
1	tsp. baking soda
1½	cups flour
¾	cup rolled oats

1. Preheat oven to 375°F.

2. Cream margarine, egg, and molasses.

3. Add remaining ingredients, stirring the oats in last.

4. Place dough by tablespoonfuls 2 inches apart on an ungreased cookie sheet.

5. Bake 8-10 minutes. The cookie will puff up, and "fall" when it is done. Remove from the oven just after it "falls." If you overbake these cookies they will be crisp . . . but not chewy.

6. Allow to stand on cookie sheet for 1-2 minutes before removing.

7. Store in a tightly covered container.

Yield: 3 dozen.

Maple-Oat Crunchies

These cookies contain no eggs or baking powder.

1½   cups rolled oats
3   cups flour
1   tsp. salt
½   cup oil
1½   cups maple syrup
2   tsp. vanilla
3   tbsp. water
1   cup raisins

1. Preheat oven to 350°F.

2. In a large bowl, mix the ingredients in the order given.

3. Drop by spoonfuls onto a lightly oiled cookie sheet.

4. Bake for 20-25 minutes.

Yield: 2-3 dozen.

Ricotta Delight

This is so easy . . . and yummy! Try to make it 12 hours in advance, to allow the graham crackers to soften and the flavors to blend.

1   lb. ricotta cheese
½   cup sugar
½   cup raisins or chopped dates
¼   cup Tia Maria or rum
6-8   Graham crackers

1.   Line serving dish with graham crackers. (A square pan works best; don't worry about the empty spaces.)

2.   Combine remaining ingredients.

3.   Pour over the graham crackers. Chill.

Yield: 4 servings.

Choco-Butter Graham Crackers

Enjoy these with milk for a super bedtime snack!

chunky peanut butter
semi-sweet chocolate chips
graham crackers

1.   Spread peanut butter on two graham crackers.

2.   Place chocolate chips on one of them. Top with the second, forming a sandwich with the inside layers of peanut butter, chocolate chips, and peanut butter.

3.   Warm in toaster-oven at low heat until the chocolate melts.

Yield: 1 serving.

Ricotta Pound Cake

I vary the filling depending on what I have handy. Raspberry jam, orange marmalade, or even cranberry sauce are nice. I like the change in texture added by chopped nuts.

Low-fat Ricotta cheese is a good source of calcium and protein.

1   **pound cake or sponge cake**
½   **lb. ricotta cheese (part skim)**
½   **cup jelly, jam, or canned fruit**

Optional:
   chopped nuts
   cinnamon
   nutmeg

1.   Slice the cake horizontally into 1-inch-thick slabs.

2.   Spread with ricotta cheese, and your choice of jelly, jam, or canned fruit. (Optional: sprinkle with cinnamon or nutmeg, and chopped nuts.)

3.   Assemble layers. Wrap in aluminum foil. Heat in oven for 25 minutes at 325°F.

Yield: 8 servings.

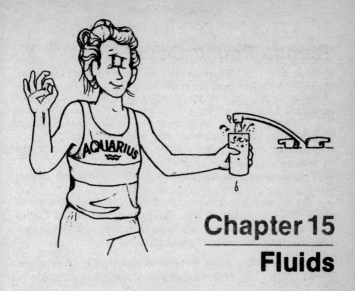

Chapter 15
Fluids

Body fluids are important: blood transports glucose to and waste products such as lactic acid from your muscles; urine eliminates waste products; sweat dissipates heat. When you exercise you can lose large amounts of water from your blood plasma. This reduces your ability to provide adequate circulation to your working muscles and to your skin for dissipating heat. This may reduce your athletic performance, and even endanger your health. To maintain adequate hydration I recommend that you routinely drink at least six to eight glasses of fluids—this includes juice, milk, and tea as well as water—each day. Drink even more on hot-weather days.

Water is Best for Replacing Losses in Sweat

Water is absorbed into your system more quickly than juices

and special electrolyte drinks that contain sugar, glucose, sodium, potassium, and other ingredients. The higher the concentration of ingredients the slower your rate of absorption. When you exercise hard for more than thirty minutes in the heat, take precautions to drink plenty of fluids.

- Bikers and hikers should carry a water bottle.
- Runners should plan a route which loops by a water fountain.
- Tennis players should take a water break between games.

In hot weather, I recommend that you drink *cold* water since it is absorbed faster. Exercise physiologist David Costill gave his research subjects 14 ounces of water at two temperatures. Here are the results:

- At 40° F., 50% of the water was absorbed in 15 minutes.
- At 95° F., 27% of the water was absorbed in 15 minutes.

Keep in mind that cold water may cool your stomach by 12-30°F. This is desireable in the heat but in the winter, hikers and skiers should try to drink warm fluids—soup, cocoa—to prevent chilling their body core. Since you generally perspire less in cold weather, the temperature of the water may be equally important to fluid replacement.

Pre-Competition Hydration

To perform at your best, you should be well saturated with water before your event.

1. Drink at least 8 glasses of fluid (8 oz. per glass) the day before.

2. Drink up to two hours before the event.

3. Drink 1-2 glasses of water five minutes before competition time.

Water Content of Food

Some fresh fruits and vegetables—such as tomatoes, celery, and lettuce—have more water (on a percentage basis) than milk or orange juice.

	% water
lettuce	95
orange	85
potato	80
hamburg	60
cheese	40
cake	20
honey	15

- When exercising rigorously in hot weather, you should ideally drink 8-10 ounces every twenty minutes. This is the amount that you can absorb from the intestines. Your body may be sweating off three times this amount; you will still have a deficit.

- Drink *before* you are thirsty. By the time your brain signals thirst you will have lost 1% of your body weight. For a 150 pound person, this is the equivalent of 1½ pounds—or three cups—of water.

- At 2% dehydration, you will have reduced your work capacity by 10-15%. Instead of running at a 7-minute pace you will be dragging along at 7:45.

Frequently, athletes ask me "Can I drink too much?" That is highly unlikely. Your kidneys will excrete the extra liquid. Drinking too little, however, is very common. You are not getting enough if you urinate infrequently, and the urine is a dark color. You may have a headache and feel irritable. Thirst does not sufficiently indicate your need for fluids. You may feel fully hydrated but still need water.

You can maintain your top performance capacity by preventing dehydration. I recommend that you weigh yourself before and after you exercise. If you have lost three pounds you should drink three pints—six cups—of fluids. (If you thought the weight you lost was fat . . . sorry! It was primarily sweat.)

After exercise, water, juice, or lemonade are fine, as are watery foods such as oranges, watermelon, cucumbers, and ice milk. You do not have to drink water, per se, to meet all of your fluid requirements.

Salt tablets are a NO-NO. They draw fluids from your body tissues to dilute the high concentration of salt in your stomach. Despite popular belief, salt tablets do not prevent muscle cramping. Cramps—although not fully understood—are possibly related to dehydration. I encourage high school football players to take plenty of water, rather than salt tablets, during their pre-season work-outs. For more information about salt, refer to the section "Shaking the Salt Habit".

Beer

"Should athletes drink beer?" is a question I am frequently asked by thirsty sports fans. I tell them that "moderation" is a key word. Drinking beer before or during an athletic event is bad because alcohol depresses your nervous system. Your brain will not function as quickly nor your muscles work as skillfully. Drinking beer immediately after an event is also unwise. Alcohol inhibits the release of an antidiuretic hormone (ADH), which retains water in the body. Instead of replacing fluids you will urinate more frequently and thus lose body fluids. After hard exercise I recommend that you first drink two to three glasses of water to replace sweat losses first. Then enjoy a few beers.

Many athletes enjoy beer as part of summertime fun.

You can easily rationalize this choice: beer is fluid, as well as nutritious, right?

I have a few questions for you to try. *True or False:*

A 12-ounce can of beer has more carbohydrates than an 8-ounce glass of orange juice.

> *False.*

	Carbohydrates	Calories
12 oz. beer	12 gms.	160
8 oz. orange juice	26 gms.	110

Beer has fewer carbohydrates but more calories. These calories come mostly from the alcohol. One gram of carbohydrate provides 4 calories. The calories in alcohol are used mainly for heat. Since you do not store them as glycogen, your muscles do not use them for energy. Do not try to replace muscle glycogen or to carbohydrate-load using beer!

True or False: A can of beer has more B-vitamins than a slice of bread.

Mostly false. Significant amounts of riboflavin (B_2) are found in beer enough to be considered nutritious. Eleven cans of beer will provide the recommended daily allowance for this one nutrient. Thiamin (B_1) is consumed by the brewer's yeast during fermentation and little is left in the finished product. Small amounts of other B-vitamins (niacin, biotin, pyridoxine, and pantothenic acid) are in beer. However, a slice of whole wheat bread, a bran muffin, or pizza will offer you more nutritional value.

Alcoholic Beverages

You can "get loaded" with alcohol, but you can't load-up your muscles with carbohydrates at the same time. The calories from beer, wine, and whiskey come mostly from the alcohol content. They are not converted into glycogen stores.

Beverage	Amount	Total Calories	Carbohydrate Calories
beer	12 oz. can	150	52
brandy, apricot	1 cordial glass	64	24
whiskey	1½ oz. jigger	105	—
wine:			
champagne	4-oz. wine glass	84	12
port	3½-oz. wine glass	158	56
sauterne	3½-oz. wine glass	84	16
vermouth, dry	3½-oz. wine glass	150	4
vermouth, sweet	3½-oz. wine glass	167	48

Source: J. Pennington and H. Church, *Bowes and Church's Food Values of Portions Commonly Used.* Harper and Row, Publishers, N.Y. 1980.

*True or False: When you've had too much beer, coffee
will have a sobering effect.*

> *False.* Coffee will simply make you a wide-awake
> drunk. The only way to get sober is to metabolize
> the alcohol. This happens in the liver at the rate of
> about one can of beer per hour. Coffee provides
> water which, once absorbed, dilutes the alcohol in
> the blood and this does have a sobering effect.

*True or False: A can of beer has more alcohol than a 1½-ounce
shot of whiskey.*

> *False.* They both have the same amount of alcohol.
> However, the alcohol in the whiskey is more
> concentrated so that it seems stronger.

Special Electrolyte Drinks

Hikers frequently ask "Should I buy special sport-drinks?"
They are concerned about choosing the best fluid replacement. It is true that you lose some electrolytes, such as
sodium and potassium, with sweat, but you do not deplete
your body stores. A normal diet supplies excessive amounts
of these electrolytes and will replace the losses. Since your
immediate need is to replace body water, not electrolytes,
special drinks are not necessary. They are costly, and also
less nutritious than natural fruit juice. For example, one cup
of Gatorade™ contains 20 milligrams of potassium, one cup
of orange juice, 500 milligrams. On a summer's day, you may
lose 320–800 milligrams of potassium during 2 hours of
strenuous exercise. The tall glass of orange juice you guzzle
afterwards supplies 800 milligrams—all that you may have
lost. Similarly a handful of pretzels or a small packet of salt
added to your next meal will replace any lost sodium.

Are You Drowning Your Thirst in Calories?

Many athletes gain weight and don't understand why. You may eat very little . . . but instead drink gallons. You probably drown your thirst in calories! Since most juices and beverages have significant amounts of calories, I suggest that you acknowledge them as being food and count their calories.

Calories/8-oz.		Calories/12-oz.	
lemonade	100	Lipton iced tea	130
grapefruit juice	100	Sprite	140
orange juice	110	Budweiser	150
apple juice	120	Pepsi	160

The best low-calorie fluid is water. If this sounds boring, some other alternatives are:

club soda with lemon	iced tea, herbal or regular
Perrier with lime	iced coffee, decaffeinated or regular

My other calorie-conscious suggestions are:

- Drink V-8 or tomato juice instead of higher-calorie fruit juices.
- Put lots of ice in your juice to dilute it.
- Flavor ice water with a little milk and almond or vanilla extract.
- Stretch red wine with club soda to make a wine spritzer.
- Reduce the amount of sugar and cream you put in your coffee. A large cup with two creamers (40 calories) and one packet of sugar (16 calories) costs you 56 calories. Your four cups per day add up to 224 calories—the caloric equivalent of a large bran muffin, or one slice of cheese pizza.

By counting the liquid calories that sneak past your lips you may discover the answer to your dietary dilemma. The calories from the can of juice or cup of coffee significantly add up. Stop to think before you drink. Would solid food give you more satisfaction than sipping fluids? If so, choose water to quench your thirst and chewable calories to appease your appetite.

Recipes for Beverages ▶

Banana Breakfast Shake
Coolie Drink
Orange Cream
Apricot Yogurt Fizz
Tea Cooler
Low-Fat Frappe
Spiced Cider
Homemade Cranberry Juice
Hot Fruit Punch

Banana Breakfast Shake

This makes a fast, nutritious, and delicious drink for breakfast or a snack.

1   cup milk
1   banana
1   tsp. vanilla
1   egg

Optional:
    ¼   cup wheat germ
    dash cinnamon
    1   tsp. honey or sugar
    4   graham crackers

1. Combine all ingredients in a blender.

2. Cover. Whirl until smooth.

Yield: 1 serving.

Coolie Drink

This will help you to beat the heat . . . and to replace potassium.

1   qt. milk
1   6-oz. can lemonade concentrate
1   1-lb. can pineapple

1. Combine all ingredients in a blender.

2. Cover. Whirl until smooth.

Yield: 4-6 servings.

Orange Cream

What a refreshing treat on a hot day! I sometimes substitute sherbert for the ice cream.

Orange juice is an excellent source of both vitamin C and potassium. Juice made from frozen concentrate is as nutritious as freshly squeezed juice.

2   cups orange juice
1   pint vanilla ice cream

Optional:
    2   eggs
    ½   cup dried milk powder
    club soda

1.   Combine orange juice and ice cream in a blender.

2.   Cover. Whirl on medium speed until smooth.

3.   Optional: fill glass two-thirds full and top it off with club soda.

Yield: 4 cups.

Apricot Yogurt Fizz

This drink tastes good with most fruits . . . use whatever you have available. It is nice either for a quick breakfast or an afternoon snack. For a more substantial beverage, or breakfast, you can add an egg.

2   canned apricot halves
8   oz. yogurt
½   cup dried milk powder
½   cup club soda

1. Combine apricots, yogurt, and dried milk in a blender.

2. Cover. Whirl on medium speed until smooth.

3. Pour into a tall glass. Add some club soda and serve immediately.

Yield: 2 cups.

Tea Cooler

A change from plain iced tea. Club soda adds a refreshing fizz.

2   cups water
3   whole cloves
1   cinnamon stick
2   tea bags
4   tbsp. orange juice, frozen concentrate
2   cups club soda

1. Heat water, cinnamon, cloves, and tea. Let stand 15 minutes. Add orange juice.

2. Pour over ice in tall glasses, leaving space to add some club soda.

3. Fill glasses with club soda and serve immediately.

Yield: 1 quart.

Low-Fat Frappe

This low-fat drink is easy to digest, which makes it a good pre-game meal.

For variety, replace the banana with strawberries or pineapple.

1   cup orange juice
1   banana
2   ice cubes
½   cup low-fat yogurt

1. Combine ingredients in a blender.

2. Cover. Whirl until smooth.

Yield: 1 serving.

Spiced Cider

Hot, spiced cider is a wonderful treat in the fall. If you make too much chill the leftover and enjoy it the next day. The flavor will be even better!

1   qt. apple cider
4   cinnamon sticks
12   cloves
1   orange, sliced into wheels

1. Combine all the ingredients in a pan.

2. Heat until boiling. Let stand a few minutes to allow the flavors to blend.

Yield: 4 servings.

Homemade Cranberry Juice

You can vary the amount of sweetness according to your preference. For variety, serve this hot.

4   **cups water**
4   **cups cranberries**
sugar, to taste

Optional:
   cinnamon stick
   whole cloves
   orange slices

1.   Cook cranberries in water until the skins pop open (about 5 minutes).

2.   Drain through a strainer lined with cloth.

3.   Bring juice to a boil. Add sugar. Boil for 2 minutes.

4.   Serve hot or chilled.

Yield: 1 quart.

Hot Fruit Punch

This beverage tastes wonderful after exercising in the cold. Make a big pot for a post-ice skating warm-up party.

Cider is a high-carbohydrate beverage. Unless it is fortified, it is not a good source of vitamin C.

2	lb. dried fruit, mixed
3	qt. water
1	cup honey or to taste
8	cinnamon sticks
20	cloves, whole
1	tsp. nutmeg
6	oranges, sliced
6	lemons, sliced
½	gal. cider

Optional:
   rum
   brandy

1. In a large pot, cook dried fruit with water for 15 minutes.

2. Stick the cloves into a whole orange. Add to the fruit.

3. Combine the remaining ingredients. Heat for 15 minutes. (Optional: if you add liquor remember that the alcohol evaporates. Don't boil it!)

Yield: 1½ gallons.

Chapter 16
Carbohydrates

Carbohydrates are the perfect energy source for fueling your muscles before and during strenuous exercise, as well as for refueling them after a hard workout. White sugar, honey, glucose, juice, and fruit are made of one type of carbohydrate: simple sugars. Pasta, rice, beans, grains, and other starches are of a second type: complex carbohydrates. The complex carbohydrates are made from chains of simple sugars. Complex carbohydrates break down during digestion into the simple sugar glucose, which is transported by the bloodstream to your working muscles. Refer to the section on "Carbohydrates: Simple vs. Complex".

Plants store carbohydrates in the form of starch. An

Glucose Is Stored In The Body

The average 150-pound male has 1800 calories of stored glucose.

	calories
muscle glycogen	1400
liver glycogen	320
blood glucose	80
Total	1800

Since training increases the amount of glycogen that you store in your muscles, trained athletes have more calories readily available for exercising.

In contrast to the limited 1800 calories from glycogen, the average man has 140,000 calories stored as fat.

Source: Felig, P. and J. Wahren., "Fuel Homeostasis in Exercise." *N. Eng. J. Med.* 293: 1079, 1975.

ear of corn, for example, is sweet when it's young but becomes starchy as it gets older. The sugar collects and is stored as starch. Humans store carbohydrates in the form of glycogen in the liver and in the muscles. This glycogen is readily available for energy. When you totally deplete your muscle glycogen by strenuously exercising for at least an hour, your muscles become inefficient. At this point, the marathoner "hits the wall" and the bicyclist "bonks". You experience extreme fatigue and struggle to slowly continue onward.

You burn mostly fat and very little glycogen when you perform light exercise, such as walking (0.3 millimoles of glycogen/kilogram/minute). When you exercise at your hardest, however, you rely primarily on glycogen (40 mM/kg./min.).

Complex carbohydrates are a nutritious as well as an inexpensive energy source. Grains, dried beans, peas, nuts, and seeds are really plant embryos. They contain the vitamins, minerals, protein, and energy essential for the first stages of plant growth. The B-vitamins that they provide are essential for metabolizing carbohydrates for fuel. Carbohydrate calories are no more fattening than the same amount of calories from protein or fat. Loading up the carbohydrates with lots of fattening fat calories is, however, a common problem. Fats are concentrated calories: one gram of fat has nine calories; one gram of carbohydrate (either sugar or starch) has four. Low carbohydrate reducing diets work only because the person eats fewer fat calories in addition to fewer carbohydrate calories. (In the chapter, "Are You Becoming an Abdominal Snowman," I will give you more information on weight control.)

For a hiker, football player, or dancer, eating a high carbohydrate meal the night before a hard workout is ideal. The meal will be fully digested; your muscle glycogen stores will be replenished and ready to provide go-power. Carbohydrates eaten less than one to two hours before the workout such as at breakfast, may just sit uncomfortably in the stomach. (Refer to the section on "Magic Meals" for information on pre-competition eating.)

Carbohydrate-loading for 2-3 days may be beneficial for endurance athletes who will be exercising hard for more than 1½-2 hours. For example, a marathoner may run longer before "hitting the wall" if the muscles are super-saturated with glycogen. In the next section, "Hungry for Success," I offer more information on carbohydrate-loading.

Chapter 17

Hungry for Success?

Pre-Competition Meals

"What's best to eat before the game?" is the question high school football players frequently ask. They hunger for that "magic meal" that insures success. I remind them that no one food or meal provides metabolic magic. Certain pre-competition eating guidelines, however, will help you to perform at your best.

Here are my answers to some recurring questions:

1. What kinds of foods should I eat?

High starch, low-fat foods are the best choice because:

- They are digested faster than protein or fat.
- They are stored in the muscles as glycogen and are readily available as energy.
- They maintain a normal blood glucose level, preventing hypoglycemia with its symptoms of weakness and light-headedness.
- They are easily digested at a time when you may be tense and/or nervous.
- Avoid sugary-sweet carbohydrates (candy, maple syrup, soda, honey). You may experience a sugar "high" that shortly will plummet to a sugar "low"—hypoglycemia. (Refer to the section on Quick Energy in Chapter 6.)
- Eat only *small* portions of low-fat protein foods. Proteins contain hard-to-digest fats that linger in your stomach. In addition, as the protein breaks down, it produces urea, a waste product that the kidneys excrete. You will need to

---

Blood Circulation During Exercise

While you exercise, your muscles need more blood to supply food and oxygen and to carry away carbon dioxide and lactic acid. Since you do not have sufficient blood to fill all of your vessels at one time, your stomach and kidneys "shut down," to allow more blood to flow to the muscles. The amount of blood that goes to the skin varies with the air temperature. In hot weather, the circulation increases as a means to cool the body and prevent overheating.

Blood flow	at rest	during hard exercise
muscles	20%	85%
digestive tract	25%	4%
kidneys	20%	3%

P. O. Astrand, *Textbook of Work Physiology.* McGraw-Hill, N.Y., 1977, p. 155.

urinate more frequently and may be inconvenienced during the competition.

Some easy-to-digest pre-game meal suggestions are:

cereal with skim milk and banana
poached egg on dry toast
peaches with low-fat cottage cheese
yogurt with applesauce and cinnamon
sliced turkey sandwich without mayonnaise
vegetable soup with crackers

2. Should I eat before a football game?

You may eat a small (less than 500 calories) pre-competition meal two to three hours before the event. Allow four to five hours for a larger meal to be digested. This period will allow you sufficient time to digest the food but not enough for your stomach to growl hungrily at you.

3. Will fluids help or hinder me before a long ski race?

Cross-country skier Amy Bennet was hesitant to drink the morning of a race because, she said, "I hate the bother of having to go to the bathroom." When I told her that dehydration can reduce athletic performance by 20–30% she agreed to experiment before a race. She drank three glasses of water two hours before. Her kidneys processed the liquid in 90 minutes so that she did not stop to urinate during the long race. "I felt extra strong. I even set a personal ski record by 4 minutes!"

I recommend that you drink at least two to three glasses of fluids two hours before the athletic event. Water and juice are fine. Coffee and tea may add to your nervousness if you are sensitive to caffeine. (Endurance athletes may choose to drink caffeine, however. See the next section for more information on caffeine.)

Since dehydration markedly reduces your athletic

performance you should enter the competition fully hydrated. Drinking extra beverages one to two days prior to the event is equally important as one to two hours beforehand.

4. Will I be regretful if I eat whatever I crave?

As the nutritionist for a regional ski team, I was surprised by the variety of pre-race breakfasts. Tom preferred to compete on an empty stomach. Peter had to have a stack of pancakes. "I don't get anywhere if I don't have my pancakes!" Both skiers raced equally well despite their different diet preferences.

I always tell my patients to choose foods that you enjoy... they may be magic to your mind. Some athletes break all of the rules and enjoy steak, pizza, or ice cream sundaes before a big event. They feel fine and compete well. Your favorite foods may have psychological powers that will work to your advantage.

5. Should I carbohydrate-load?

The average tennis player, cyclist, jogger, and athlete who exercises hard for less than ninety non-stop minutes has sufficient glycogen to meet his or her energy demands. A carbohydrate-rich meal, such as spaghetti or tuna-noodle casserole, the night before the football game or ten kilometer road race will sufficiently saturate your muscles with glycogen. You will not benefit from extended loading for two to three days prior to the event.

Want to Load Up?

Before the 1980 Boston Marathon, Bob Goldstein came to me. "Do you recommend that I load-up on carbohydrates? I don't want to change my normal vegetarian diet unless you think that it will really help."

I told Bob that some exercise physiologists are questioning the benefits of the traditional week long deplete-and-load regimen. "They seem to think that, for a highly trained athlete, loading is sufficient."

Some marathon runners, cross-country ski racers, long distance bicyclists and other endurance athletes carbo-hydrate-load by following this schedule the week prior to the event:

	Exercise	Diet
Sunday	Exhaustive — to deplete glycogen	Low carbohydrate — to limit glycogen storage
Monday Tuesday	Moderate — to maintain depletion	
Wednesday Thursday Friday	Light — to rest the muscles and to limit glycogen utilization	High carbohydrate — to super-saturate glycogen stores
Saturday	Go for it!	High carbohydrate — afterwards, to replace glycogen

With hard training, you repeatedly deplete your glycogen stores and re-load them when you next eat. Depletion stimulates greater glycogen repletion. Your "starved" muscles super-saturate themselves above the initial glycogen level. I remind my patients that hard (i.e., short, intense or longer, less-intense) training work-outs are

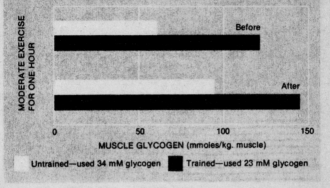

Glycogen stores increase with training

MODERATE EXERCISE FOR ONE HOUR

Before

After

| 0 | 50 | 100 | 150 |

MUSCLE GLYCOGEN (mmoles/kg. muscle)

Untrained—used 34 mM glycogen   Trained—used 23 mM glycogen

Training increases your ability to store more glycogen in your muscles. Training also increases your ability to use less glycogen—and more fat— as an energy source. Hence, trained athletes use less glycogen. One reason you can exercise longer is because you take longer to use all the glycogen. [1]

conducive to optimal glycogen storage. A high carbohydrate diet without prior glycogen depletion will saturate—but not super-saturate—your muscles.

Most elite athletes realize that training is equally important to diet for increasing the amount of glycogen stored in the muscles.

gm. glycogen/100 gm. muscle

untrained muscle	13
trained muscle	32
"loaded" muscle	35-40

[1] Evans, W. et. al. "Leg Muscle Metabolism in Trained and Un-trained Men." *Res. Quart.* 50:350, 1979.

Calories from Carbohydrates

	% carbohydrate-calories
sugar	100
orange juice	100
fig bar	85
pasta	82
bread	79
pancakes, syrup	70
chocolate bar	43
ice cream	41
peanut butter	15
cheese	2

The remaining calories come from protein and fat.

Based on: J. Pennington and H. Church. *Bowes and Church's Food Values of Portions Commonly Used.* Harper and Row, Publishers, N.Y., 1980.

Elite athletes, Bill Rodgers for example, eat high carbohydrate foods for two to three days prior to a marathon. They generally do not carry out the depletion phase of carbohydrate-loading because they want to rest their muscles. When athletes who are preparing for an endurance event ask me for advice, I give them these tips for loading-up:

1. Plan your pre-marathon menu. Choose high carbohydrate foods and do *not* confuse them with high fat foods, such as pepperoni pizza, ice cream, cheese cake, fudge, and Danish pastry. Fatty foods taste good and will fatten you up, but they won't maximally fill your muscles with glycogen. Only carbohydrates are readily converted into muscle glycogen.

2. Eat primarily carbohydrates for two to four days beforehand.

3. Eat a very high carbohydrate dinner the night beforehand. I suggest that you moderately over-eat rather than slightly under-eat. You may wish to include bran bread and other high-fiber foods to prevent constipation problems.

I recommend that you choose from the foods that are highest in carbohydrates and low in fat.

Foods highest in carbohydrates:	Comments:
Spaghetti, macaroni, noodles	Tomato sauce is carbohydrate; the meat, cheese, and oil are not . . . eat them in moderation.
Rice	Steamed or boiled rice is fine; fried rice has too much oil.
Potato, stuffing	Add only small amounts of butter, gravy, or soured cream. *No* french fries.
Starchy vegetables—such as peas, carrots, winter squash, yams	Lots of vitamins and minerals along with the carbohydrates.
Chili beans, lentils, split pea soup, lima beans, baked beans	All dried beans and peas are high in carbohydrates. Caution: eating large portions may lead to digestive problems.
Bread, rolls, crackers	Enriched whole wheat, bran, and dense breads are nutritionally better than white bread.
Banana bread, date-nut bread	
Muffins, cornbread, bagels	Spread with honey, jelly, or jam instead of butter or cream cheese.
Hot cereals, such as oatmeal, Cream of Wheat™, Wheatena™ Cold cereals, such as Grape-nuts ™, Raisin Bran, MOST™	Add raisins, banana, or canned fruit. Choose dense, rather than puffed or flaked cereals. Note: serve with low-fat milk.
Pancakes, waffles	Serve with syrup, jam, or honey. Use butter sparingly.

Foods highest in carbohydrates:	Comments:
Fresh and canned fruits, such as bananas, pineapple	Dense, rather than watery fruits, have more carbohydrates.
Dried fruits, such as raisins, dates	Beware: eating large amounts may cause diarrhea.
Low-fat desserts, such as fig bars, apple crisp, peach cobbler	Most cakes and cookies are made with a lot of shortening, and offer mainly fat calories.
Juices: apple, pineapple, cranberry, peach, pear, apricot nectar	Orange and grapefruit have fewer carbohydrates than sweeter juices.
Lemonade, Kool-Aid™, soda	Not as healthful as natural juice.
Fruit smoothie: fruit and juice mixed in the blender	Frozen orange juice concentrate makes a good base.
Low-fat yogurt with fruit	Buy flavored yogurt or make your own by adding fruit or jam.
Sherbert, ice milk	Better than ice cream.
Jelly beans, gum drops, marshmallows, honey, jelly, jam, syrup	Pure sugar, with little nutritional value, but lots of carbohydrates.

Pasta, potato, rice, bread, and other starchy foods are equally effective as honey, raisins, gumdrops, and juice for making glycogen. The starches have more nutritional value, however, and will provide important vitamins and minerals in addition to the glycogen.

When you load up on carbohydrates you will also increase your body's water supply. With each gram of

---

A 3800-Calorie Carbohydrate-Loading Diet

This sample diet is not only high in carbohydrates, but also high in fiber. The competing athlete does not want to be constipated.

	Calories	% Carbohydrate
8 oz. orange juice	110	93
½ cup Grape-nuts	210	88
1 medium banana	140	94
8 oz. low-fat milk	110	48
1 whole wheat English muffin	130	83
1 tbsp. jelly	50	100
2 oz. turkey, sliced	155	—
2 sl. bran bread	175	74
lettuce/tomato	25	83
8 oz. apple juice	120	100
1 cup lemon sherbert	275	91
3 cup spaghetti (6 oz. uncooked)	625	82
½ cup tomato sauce with		
mushrooms	75	64
2 tbsp. parmesan cheese	55	—
¼ loaf French bread	300	75
1 cup apple crisp with	400	82
¼ cup raisins	130	97
16 oz. cranberry juice	290	100
6 fig cookies	330	80
Total calories = 3815		80% carbohydrate calories

glycogen you store three grams of water. You will gain water weight as you load-up . . . this is one indication that you are eating right. You release this water as you burn the glycogen, and it will aid in reducing the dangers of dehydration. You won't starve to death during a grueling endurance event, but you may become seriously disabled for lack of water. I encourage my patients to drink plenty of fluids for two to three days beforehand to assure maximal hydration. Remember that large amounts of beer, wine and alcohol are dehydrating. Alcohol inhibits the release of a water-retaining hormone ADH; this causes you to urinate more frequently and lose body fluids. You may enjoy a little wine or beer to relax, but I recommend drinking mostly water and juice. Do not try to carbohydrate-load with beer.

On the morning of the race drink at least two to three glasses of water. Allow two hours before race time for the

Sixty minutes before exercising, the subjects took caffeine equivalent to two cups of coffee. They exercised 19% longer before reaching exhaustion.

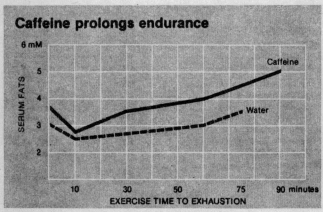

Caffeine prolongs endurance

Costill, D. "Effects of Caffeine Ingestion on Metabolism and Exercise Performance." *Med. Sci. Sports* 10: 155-158, 1978.

kidneys to process this fluid. Drink another glass five to ten minutes before starting time. Since the kidneys essentially "shut down" during strenuous activity this final water will remain in your system.

"What about coffee . . . will the caffeine improve my marathon time?" runner Dick Babson asked me when I was giving him dietary advice for his first marathon. "Coffee may help you run longer without 'hitting the wall,' and may even help you run a bit faster." I explained the research studies by David Costill. In one study the subjects drank two cups of coffee (330 mg. caffeine) one hour before strenuous exercise. They worked for 15 minutes longer than when tested without the caffeine (see left below).

In a second study the subjects took 250 mg. caffeine both before and during exercise. They cycled for two hours on a special bicycle that recorded the amount of energy they expended. In the two-hour period, the subjects cycled 7% harder when they took the caffeine but perceived the effort as being the same (see below).

The subjects who took caffeine equivalent to two cups of coffee worked 7% harder, yet perceived the effort to be no harder.

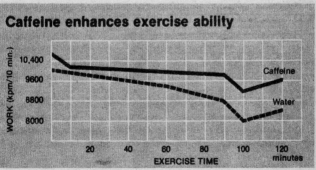

Ivy, J., Costill, D., "Influence of Caffeine and Carbohydrate Feedings on Endurance Performance." *Med. Sci. Sports* 11:6, 1979.

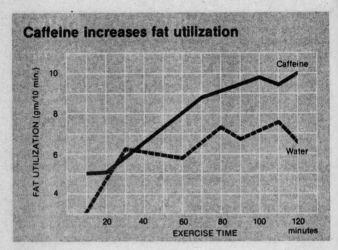

Caffeine increases fat utilization

Caffeine stimulates your body to release fats into the blood. Your muscles prefer to burn the fats and spare the glycogen. This helps you to exercise longer. In a two-hour period these subjects worked 7% harder and burned 31% more fat. [1]

If you chose to drink coffee before endurance exercise two cups will do the trick for a 150-pound person. Lightweight athletes—or those sensitive to caffeine—should drink less. Caffeine overdose is common with athletes who drink three to four large mugs of coffee before competition. They become so hyper that they perform poorly. Contrary to common belief, caffeine's stimulant effect is NOT responsible for prolonging endurance performance. Rather caffeine reduces the rate at which you burn glycogen. Caffeine stimulates the release of fats from the tissues into the bloodstream. As more fats become available your

[1] Ivy, J. et al. "Influence of Caffeine and Carbohydrate Feedings on Endurance Performance." *Med. Sci. Sports* 11:6, 1979.

muscles burn these instead of the glycogen. You are able to comfortably exercise longer before you deplete your limited glycogen stores, "hit the wall," and feel totally exhausted. For more information about coffee and caffeine, I suggest that you turn back to the section "Does Coffee Keep You Perking?" in Chapter 4.

Recovery

After his 50-kilometer cross-country ski race, Bill Thompson couldn't wait for his thick steak dinner. "I'm ready for some meat. I'm tired of pasta!" He wasn't aware that he still

After performing exhaustive exercise that depleted their glycogen, the subjects ate either: (a) a high carbohydrate diet, which refilled the glycogen in two days, or (b) a high protein, high fat diet, which left the glycogen stores unfilled, even after five days.

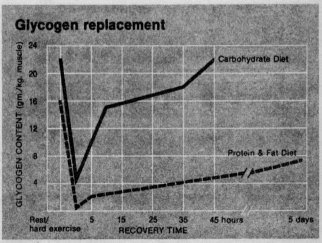

Bergstrom, J., et al. "Diet, Muscle Glycogen and Physical Performance." *Acta Physiol. Scand.* 71:140, 1967.

needed carbohydrates to re-load his hard-worked muscles. For a speedy recovery, I recommend that you keep eating carbohydrates just as you did before the event to rapidly refill your empty glycogen stores. When you celebrate your victory, remember that pasta, bread, fruit, and juice are still the best choices. Save the steak for another day.

Potassium is stored along with glycogen, so you will want to meet this need, which is easy to do. Potassium is found in most foods, especially fruits and vegetables. The average American diet contains a substantial 4000-6000 milligrams of potassium. You need 3000 milligrams normally, with an additional 1000 milligrams when putting down glycogen. To insure that you meet your needs, I recommend that you choose foods to eat from the following excellent sources:

High potassium foods	mg. potassium
orange juice, 1 cup	380
banana, 1 medium	550
raisins, ½ cup	760
apricots, dried, ½ cup	980
spinach, cooked, ½ cup	325
carrots, raw, 1 large	340
potato, with skin, 1 medium	450
winter squash, ½ cup	415

Chapter 18

Is Gaining Weight
A Losing Battle?

"I can never gain weight. If I were to eat all day I still wouldn't add any fat to my bones" complained cyclist Frank LeBeau. When I analyzed Frank's diet I clearly saw why he didn't gain weight. He used little butter or margarine and no salad dressing. He drank water with his meals and he didn't snack. His meals were seemingly huge. However, he filled up on bulky low-calorie fruits and vegetables rather than on foods with concentrated calories.

Gaining weight, or maintaining an ideal weight throughout a strenuous sports season is a problem for many athletes. The solution is clear-cut and mathematical: to gain one pound in one week you must consume an extra 500 calories each day that you do not expend. You can do this by:

- eating an extra snack, such as a peanut butter sandwich and a glass of milk.
- eating larger portions or second helpings at meals.
- choosing higher-calorie foods, for example, banana instead of grapefruit.

Before starting a weight-gain program, I ask my patients why they want to gain weight. For the most part, extra fat is an unnecessary burden. It steals energy that your muscles could use. If you want to gain weight for cosmetic reasons and will think better about yourself, then weight-gain may be beneficial.

Weighty Information

If you want to gain a few pounds the following weighty information will help you reach your goal:

1. Determine your daily caloric needs. This is approximately 17 calories per pound if you perform only light activity. A nutritionist can more accurately calculate this information based on your height, weight, age, sex, and activity. Add an extra 500 calories to gain one pound in a week; 1000 calories to gain two pounds in a week.

2. Write down everything that you eat and drink for three days. A nutritionist can calculate the number of calories that you are presently eating, or you can use a calorie guidebook. I recommend a readily available paperback *Calories and Carbohydrates* by Barbara Kraus, or the more complete *Bowes and Churchs' Food Values of Portions Commonly Used* by J. Pennington and H. Church.

3. Trade lower-calorie foods for ones with more calories. Use a calorie guide book to become familiar with the caloric value of the foods and include higher-calorie choices in your diet. For example, grape juice has more calories than orange juice; granola has more than Raisin Bran. Misinformation may fool you: a 12-ounce can of beer is generally considered fattening, but the same amount of milk offers 80 more calories—and a lot more nutritional value!

4. Focus on polyunsaturated fats—a concentrated source of calories. Eat toast with corn oil margarine, salads with safflower oil-based dressing, and thick sandwiches made with old-fashioned peanut butter. I recommend that you eat saturated animal fats (butter, ice cream, cheese, and meats) in moderation. A high saturated fat-high cholesterol diet will contribute to weight gain, and also to heart disease. I believe that your overall health is equally important to your sports career. The section on "What About Cholesterol?" discusses this topic in more detail. Fruits, juices, and vegetables—although a nutritious part of your diet—provide filling bulk without a lot of calories. Include them in moderate amounts. Dried fruits—raisins, dates—and starchy vegetables—yams, winter squash—are the best choices.

5. Plan your heaviest meals or snacks for when you will have time to digest them whether it is breakfast, dinner, or bedtime. Eat until you feel full then eat a bit more. For you, food may be like medicine that you must force yourself to take.

6. Exercise vigorously. A regular training program in addition to a high-calorie diet will help you to gain muscle instead of just fat. Routinely evaluate your progress by having a nutritionist measure your skinfold and your weight.

Boost Your Calories

Small changes in your normal eating habits can make big changes in your weight. Compare these two diets:

	Usual Choices	calories
Breakfast	8 oz. orange juice	110
	1½ cup bran flakes	200
	8 oz. milk	160
	1 sl. toast	80
	1 pat margarine	50
	½ tbsp. jelly	30
	1 cup coffee	0
Lunch	Quarter-pound hamburg	420
	large fries	215
	large cola	160
Snack	large apple	130
Dinner	1 cup vegetable soup	80
	7 oz. chicken, baked	330
	1 cup potato, mashed	150
	1 pat margarine	50
	1 cup green beans	40
	½ pat margarine	25
	½ cup jello	70
	8 oz. milk	160
Snack	8 oz. tomato juice	40
	1 English muffin	130
	1 pat margarine	50
	1 tbsp. honey	60
	Total Calories	2740

Source: Nancy Clark, M.S., R.D., Sports Medicine Resource, Inc., Boston, MA.

High-calorie Choices	calories
8 oz. cranberry juice	170
1½ cup granola	780
8 oz. milk with ¼ cup dried milk	220
1 sl. toast	80
1 pat margarine	50
2 tbsp. peanut butter	190
1 cup hot cocoa	225
Quarter-pound cheeseburger	550
large fries	215
chocolate shake	360
large banana	170
1 cup split pea soup	130
7 oz. chicken, baked	330
1 cup noodles	200
2 pats margarine	100
2 tbsp. parmesan cheese	110
1 cup corn	140
1 pat margarine	50
1 cup pudding	200
8 oz. milk with ¼ cup dried milk	220
8 oz. pineapple juice	150
1 English muffin	130
2 pats margarine	100
2 oz. cheese	200
Total Calories	5040

The small changes contributed 2300 extra calories. One pound of fat contains 3500 calories.

Chapter 19

Are You Becoming An Abdominal Snowman?

If creeping obesity is changing FIT into FAT, today is the day to stop "waisting" your health. Excess pounds:

- stress your heart
- burden your back
- tire your feet
- reduce your athletic agility

- tarnish your self-image
- contribute to diabetes, heart disease, and
    hypertension

To lose weight you need a positive state of mind and a commitment to your gratifying goal. You must remember that it is okay to be hungry. One of my patients used to panic for food whenever she felt hungry. I told her, "Think of your hunger as a sign of success. It means that you are following your diet. You're getting lighter, running stronger, and feeling fitter." I also tell my patients that extreme hunger is not healthful. When you drastically reduce your food intake you also reduce your vitamin and mineral intake. You need to eat daily at least 1200 calories from a variety of nutritious foods to get the fundamental forty nutrients that your body requires for maintaining your health and meeting your athletic demands.

The two keys to successful weight loss are:

1. Eat less.
2. Exercise more.

Losing weight is mathematical: one pound of fat is the equivalent of 3500 calories of stored energy. By eating 500 less calories than you burn each day you will lose one pound in a week. Some of my patients think that certain foods burn off extra calories or that special machines will jiggle away the fat. The only way to lose fat is to eat less calories than you expend.

Dietary Do's

If you have made the mental commitment to lose weight I recommend the following suggestions to help you reach and maintain your goal:

1. Determine your ideal weight based on your percentage of body fat. The best and most convenient way to measure body fat is with a skin-fold caliper. This instrument works on the principle that fat is stored underneath the skin. The more fat you have, the thicker the layer. By pinching the thickness of the layer, the caliper measures your body fat.

Six-foot tall 160-pound runner Ted Rosen wishfully told me, "I'd like to weigh 150 pounds. That seems to be the ideal weight for a marathoner." "Most runners are smaller than you, Ted. You need to weigh more since you have additional muscle and bone. Let me figure our your ideal weight." Using skin-fold calipers, I calculated his percentage of body fat. It

was 7% . . . an excellent level for a long distance runner.

A nutritionist can best determine your ideal weight by measuring your body fat. Popular height-weight charts are inappropriate for athletes because they provide little information regarding the composition of your body weight. Muscle is 22½% denser than fat. A muscular 180-pound cyclist may be over-weight according to the standards, but he will not be over-fat.

You need a certain amount of body fat to maintain your health. Women have more essential fat than men so they can nurture a child. A woman who becomes too thin stops producing the hormones for menstruating; thus Mother Nature protects her from the possibility of bearing an unhealthy baby.

Body Fat:	Male	Female
Essential	3%	13%
Average person	15-18	25-28
Athlete	10-15	16-20
Elite Athlete	5-8	13-16

A less professional method to check your body fat is the "mirror test." If you *see* fat when you stand naked in front of a mirror, then you *are* fat.

2. Be realistic with your time frame. I allot my patients one week to lose two pounds; four to five weeks to lose ten pounds. I want slow and steady weight loss which represents fat loss. Quick loss represents mostly water and muscle wasting. In addition, you may feel weak and perform poorly. A wrestler who "makes weight" but loses the match is a detriment to the team.

3. Reject fad diets. Claims for "all you can eat," "no will power," or "spot reduction" rarely hold true. There is no quick and easy way to lose weight. Fad diets are unbalanced, unrealistic, and unhealthy since:

- They generally eliminate important food groups such as carbohydrates—an important part of an athlete's diet. This will also eliminate certain vitamins and minerals.

- They drastically reduce your caloric intake to an unliveable, unrealistic level. You may lose your pleasant personality more than your fat.

- They promote muscle deterioration and water loss more than fat loss. In "starvation" conditions your muscles break down to provide energy and you want them for exercising!

Athletes who try to lose weight by fasting and dehydration compromise both their health and their performance.

Gymnast Marsha Banks came to me after attempting a 500-calorie crash diet. "I was starving all the time and my practice sessions were awful. I managed to stay on the diet for four days. I told my family to stay away from me because I was so irritable. In fact, they were the ones who finally encouraged me to come to you for professional guidance." With my advice Marsha reached her goal in five weeks. "This has been the only diet that has worked for me . . . and

I've been able to enjoy my favorite foods and still lose weight." Marsha learned that fad diets teach you how to diet but not how to eat and maintain your strength.

4. Eat smaller portions. Continue to enjoy the foods that you normally eat, but enjoy smaller amounts. For example:

- half of a pizza instead of the whole
- a small ice cream cone instead of the sundae

You will get half of the calories but have the full enjoyment of choosing what you want. By eating 500 calories less than you burn each day, you will lose a pound in a week.

Weight watcher Janet Rhodes used to eat primarily grapefruit, cottage cheese, eggs, and salads. She would be content with this limited selection until she experienced a stressful day. When Janet began to feel sorry for herself she'd buy her favorite treat—an ice cream sundae. No wonder her diets were never successful.

By eating the foods that you normally enjoy, you will feel psychologically satisfied rather than denied. The "I feel sorry for myself" syndrome is a dietary disaster.

The total number of calories per day not the source of the calories determines the amount of weight you lose. Two hundred calories from cottage cheese are just as fattening as two hundred calories from bread. The popular high protein diets do not induce weight loss. If that were true the Eskimos, who eat little but fish and blubber, would have wasted away centuries ago. They eat sufficient high protein calories to maintain their weight.

I encourage my patients to measure their food since the portion size is critical. A *level* ½ cup of rice has 70 calories; a *heaping* ½ cup has 115 calories. A *level* ½ cup of cottage cheese has 110 calories; a *heaping* ½ cup has 135 calories. You fool only yourself by sneaking a few extra mouthfuls.

5. Choose more fruits, vegetables, and low-fat foods. Creamy, greasy, and fatty foods are the caloric culprits. Fat in any form is concentrated calories, a store of energy. Thus to lose weight, you should limit your intake of:

butter	cream cheese	fried food
margarine	peanut butter	fatty meat
oil	soured cream	gravy
salad dressing	mayonnaise	sauces

Beware of hidden fats in cheese, meat, nuts, and bakery items.

6. Eat at regular times. Skipping meals frequently leads to over-compensating at the end of the day when you feel uncontrollably ravenous. The pizza at 10 P.M. that you claim you deserve is more fattening than the breakfast and lunch that you skipped. Based on 6 years of experience, I've found that most overweight people frequently skip breakfast and/or lunch.

Energy Expended in Various Activities

Energy expenditure by a 150-pound person in various activities*:

Activity	Calories per Hour
A. Rest and Light Activity	50-200
lying down or sleeping	80
sitting	100
driving an automobile	120
standing	140
domestic work	180
B. Moderate Activity	200–350
bicycling (5½ mph)	210
walking (2½ mph)	210
gardening	220
canoeing (2½ mph)	230
golf	250
lawn mowing (power mower)	250
bowling	270
lawn mowing (hand mower)	270
fencing	300
rowboating (2½ mph)	300
swimming (¼ mph)	300
walking (3¾ mph)	300
badminton	350
horseback riding (trotting)	350
square dancing	350
volleyball	350
roller skating	350
C. Vigorous Activity	over 350
table tennis	360
ditch digging (hand shovel)	400
ice skating (10 mph)	400
wood chopping or sawing	400
tennis	420
water skiing	480
hill climbing (100 ft. per hr.)	490
skiing (10 mph)	600

squash and handball	600
bicycling (13 mph)	660
scull rowing (race)	840
running (10 mph)	900

*The standards represent a compromise between those proposed by the British Medical Association (1950), Christensen (1953), and Wells, Balke, and Van Fossan (1956). Where available, actual measured values have been used; for other values a "best guess" was made.

Source: Robert E. Johnson, M.D., Ph.D., Professor of Biology, Knox College, Coordinator, Knox Rush Medical Program, Scientific Consultant, Department of Medicine, Presbyterian St. Lukes Hospital, Chicago.

7. Exercise more. The more active you are the more calories you burn. Exercise:

- expends calories
- promotes fat loss
- tones your muscles
- strengthens your heart
- trims inches
- increases your body awareness
- improves your self-image

In addition to your daily training incorporate new ways to step up your energy output. Walk to the post office, park your car at the far end of the lot, take an exercise break instead of a coffee break, use the stairs instead of the elevator.

Since I get little exercise at work I plan to be inefficient. For example, I will write a letter and take it to the mail room. Then I will write another letter and walk a second time to the mail room. My office mates think I'm forgetful, but I enjoy the extra exercise.

8. Quench your thirst with water. Sweaty athletes guzzle lots of liquids containing lots of calories. If you convert these calories into solid food, you easily see them as fattening additions to your diet.

- One quart of orange juice is equal in calories to a peanut butter sandwich.
- Two cans of Coke are equivalent to a large ice cream cone.
- One beer is the equivalent of six cups of unbuttered popcorn.

Water is readily available, low-calorie, and low cost. It is the best diet drink for athletes. (See the section on Fluids for more information about sweat replacement.)

Losing Weight but Lacking Energy?

Athletes who diet frequently lack energy resulting from an inadequate intake of carbohydrates. Carbohydrates are an important part of a reduction diet and they have fewer calories than protein foods. For example:

1 slice wheat bread	=	80 calories
2 tbsp. peanut butter	=	190 calories
½ cup mashed potato	=	90 calories
½ cup cottage cheese	=	120 calories

Weight for weight, an ounce of carbohydrate (either sugar or starch) has half the calories of fats. Fat combines with protein and converts it into a high-calorie choice for the dieter.

carbohydrate	4 calories/gm.
protein	4
fat	9

Carbohydrates—and only carbohydrates—quickly replace the muscle glycogen you burn during exercise. If you train hard while eating a low-calorie low-carbohydrate diet, you will feel tired and sluggish. Each day you will further deplete your muscle glycogen stores. A diet that contains mostly protein and fat, but limited carbohydrates will not replenish the muscle glycogen. Instead, eat higher carbohydrate foods for each meal, for example:

Breakfast: cereal, low-fat milk, and juice, instead of eggs

Lunch: yogurt, fruit, and crackers, instead of cottage cheese and a salad

Dinner: tuna-noodle casserole and broccoli, instead of baked chicken

David Costill's research indicates the importance of eating carbohydrates on those days you exercise repeatedly. He studied trained subjects who ran for ten miles (6- to 8-minute pace) for three consecutive days. They ate a diet that provided about half of the calories from carbohydrates. Despite this moderate carbohydrate intake, the muscles remained partially depleted.

To perform best while you are dieting, you should eat moderate amounts of fruit, juice, bread, potatoes, crackers, vegetables, and other carbohydrates. Eat less fatty meats and foods with mayonnaise, margarine, butter, and salad

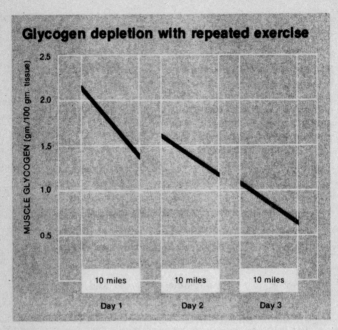

Glycogen depletion with repeated exercise

Exercise physiologist David Costill studied the rate of muscle glycogen depletion in five subjects who ran for 10 miles (6–8 minute mile pace) on three consecutive days. The runners ate their normal diet, which provided 40% to 60% of the calories from carbohydrates. They continually depleted, but did not replenish, the muscle glycogen.

Based on this information, you can understand why:

• *Carbohydrates are important for athletes who train every day; and why*
• *Carbohydrates are an important part of an athlete's reducing diet.*

Costill, D. et al. "Muscle Glycogen Utilization During Prolonged Exercise on Successive Days." *J. Appl. Physiol.* 31:834, 1971.

dressing. The fats are most fattening and least beneficial to your muscles or your reduction diet.

Learning to follow a diet is less important than learning how to eat for a lifetime. You will be better off to trade in your fattening dietary problems for healthful habits. A nutritionist can teach you how to eat wisely, lose weight, and maintain that weight loss. Good nutrition is an investment in your present performance as well as in your future health.

Appendix A: Herbs and Spices

Do herbs and spices mystify you? I used to avoid them because I was afraid of adding an undesirable flavor to the food. Now I have learned to use them creatively. Spices:

- add appealing new flavor to wearisome foods. For example, I sprinkle some oregano on my "plain ol' cheese sandwich."
- are an effective salt substitute. I add curry powder in place of half the salt to some of my soups.

When you try a new seasoning, I suggest that you experiment cautiously. Once you have over-seasoned there is little you can do except to double the recipe. I have given some tips to help you get started with creative cookery:

- Start with ¼ tsp. dry herbs (or ¾ tsp. fresh herbs) for a dish that serves four people.
- Crumble the herbs between your fingers to release the flavor.
- Heat the herbs in oil to heighten and extend their flavor.
- With soups, stews, and large cooking dishes, add the herbs during the last hour.
- Store herbs in a cool place to retain their flavor—NOT near the stove.
- Routinely replace your supply.
- Ground spices retain their flavor for about six months. Herbs dry out after four months.

Some harmonious combinations are:

basil	tomato dishes, salads, fish
marjoram	fish, meat, poultry, stuffing
oregano	tomato dishes, fish, salads
parsley	soups, salads, vegetables, garnish
poppy seeds	cottage cheese, noodles, cole slaw
rosemary	fish, meat, poultry, stuffing, vegetables
sage	soups, stews, stuffing
thyme	tomato dishes, stews, salads, vegetables
cinnamon	cooked fruits, winter squash, baked goods
clove	hot cider or tea, cooked fruits, tomatoes, winter squash
ginger	cooked fruits, curry, chicken
nutmeg	apple desserts, puddings, winter squash

Tried and true combinations:

oregano and marjoram
oregano and rosemary
cinnamon and nutmeg
ginger and clove
thyme and parsley
sage and parsley

Appendix B: Weights and Measures

3 teaspoons (tsp.)	=	1 tablespoon (tbsp.)
2 tablespoons	=	1 liquid ounce or ⅛ cup
4 tablespoons	=	¼ cup
8 tablespoons	=	½ cup
16 tablespoons	=	1 cup
1 cup	=	½ pint (8 ounces)
2 cups	=	1 pint (16 ounces)
4 tablespoons flour	=	1 ounce
4 cups flour	=	1 pound
2 cups white sugar	=	1 pound
2 2/3 cups confectioners sugar	=	1 pound
2 2/3 cups brown sugar	=	1 pound

Appendix C: Approximate Compostion of Common Food Fats

	Choles-terol/ tbsp.	% Polyun-saturated	% Mono-un-saturated	% Satu-rated
Oils:				
coconut	0	0	8	92
corn	0	58	31	11
cottonseed	0	59	16	25
olive	0	7	81	12
peanut	0	31	46	23
safflower	0	78	12	10
soybean	0	63	21	16
hydrogenated soybean	0	37	49	14
sunflower	0	53	15	12
Special Margarine:				
Chiffon™	0	55	31	14
Fleisch-mann's™	0	33	48	19
Mazola™	0	34	46	20

	Choles-terol/tbsp.	%Polyun-saturated	%Mono-un-saturated	%Satu-rated
Fats:				
butter	30	4	37	59
lard	1	10	52	38
Crisco™	0	26	49	25
regular hydrog-enated shortening	0	7	70	23

Source: Sylvia Rosenthal. *Live High on Low Fat.* Harper & Row/Lippincott Co., Philadelphia, 1968.

Appendix D: Vitamin Facts

Vitamins	U.S. RDA for Adults and Children over four	Some Significant Sources
Fat-Soluble Vitamins		
Vitamin A *(retinol, provitamin carotenoids)*	5000 I.U.	*Retinol:* liver, butter, whole milk, cheese, egg yolk. *Pro-vitamin A:* carrots, leafy green vegetables, sweet potatoes, pumpkin, squash, apricots, cantaloupe, fortified margarine.
Vitamin D *(calciferol)*	400 I.U.	Vitamin D fortified dairy products; fortified margarine; fish oils; egg yolk. Synthesized by sunlight action on skin.

Some Major Physiological Functions	Some Deficiency Symptoms	Some Overconsumption Symptoms
Assists formation and maintenance of skin and mucous membranes, thus increasing resistance to infections. Functions in visual processes and forms visual purple. Promotes bone and tooth development.	**Mild:** night-blindness, diarrhea, intestinal infections, impaired growth. *Severe:* xerophthalmia.	**Mild:** nausea, irritability, blurred vision. *Severe:* growth retardation, enlargement of liver and spleen, loss of hair, rheumatic pain, increased pressure in skull, dermal changes.
Promotes ossification of bones and teeth, increases intestinal absorption of calcium.	Rickets in children; osteomalacia in adults, rare.	**Mild:** nausea, weight loss, irritability. *Severe:* mental and physical growth retardation, kidney damage, mobilization of calcium from bony tissue and deposition in soft tissues. *(continued)*

Vitamins	U.S. RDA for Adults and Children over four	Some Significant Sources
Fat-Soluble Vitamins		
Vitamin E *(tocopherol)*	30 I.U.	Vegetable oil, margarine, shortening; green and leafy vegetables; wheat germ, whole grain products; egg yolk; butter, liver.
Water-Soluble Vitamins		
Vitamin C *(ascorbic acid)*	60 mg.	Broccoli, sweet and hot peppers, collards, brussels sprouts, strawberries; orange, kale, grapefruit, papaya, potato, mango, tangerine, spinach, tomato.
Thiamin *(vitamin B₁)*	1.5 mg.	Pork, liver, meat; whole grains, fortified grain products; legumes; nuts.
Riboflavin *(vitamin B₂)*	1.7 mg.	Liver; milk, yogurt, cottage cheese; meat; fortified grain products.

Some Major Physiological Functions	Some Deficiency Symptoms	Some Overconsumption Symptoms
Functions as antioxidant protecting vitamins A and C and fatty acids from destruction, and prevents cell-membrane damage.	Almost impossible to produce without starvation; possible anemia in low-birth-weight infants.	Nontoxic under normal conditions.
Forms cementing substances, such as collagen, that hold body cells together, thus strengthening blood vessels, hastening healing of wounds and bones, and increasing resistance to infection. Aids in use of iron.	**Mild:** bruise easily, bleeding gums. *Severe:* scurvy.	Nontoxic under normal conditions. When megadose is discontinued, deficiency symptoms may briefly appear until the body adapts.
Functions as part of a coenzyme to promote carbohydrate metabolism, production of ribose, a constituent of DNA and RNA. Promotes normal appetite and normal functioning of nervous system.	Impaired growth, wasting of tissues, mental confusion, low morale, edema. *Severe:* beriberi.	Infants whose mothers ingested megadoses during pregnancy will show deficiency symptoms after birth until the body adapts.
Functions as part of a coenzyme assisting cells to use oxygen for the release of energy from food. Promotes good vision and healthy skin.	Lesions of cornea, cracks at corners of mouth.	None reported. *(continued)*

Vitamins	U.S. RDA for Adults and Children over four	Some Significant Sources
Water-Soluble Vitamins		
Niacin *(nicotinamide, nicotinic acid)*	20 mg.	Liver, meat, poultry, fish; peanuts; fortified grain products. Synthesized from tryptophan on the average 1 mg. of niacin from 60 mg. of dietary tryptophan.
Folacin *(folic acid)*	0.4 mg.	Liver; legumes; green leafy vegetables.
Vitamin B$_6$ *(pyridoxine, pyridoxal, pyridoxamine)*	2.0 mg.	Meat, poultry, fish, shellfish; green and leafy vegetables; whole grains, legumes.
Vitamin B$_{12}$	6.0 mcg.	Meat, poultry, fish, shellfish; eggs; milk and milk products.

Courtesy: National Dairy Council.

Some Major Physiological Functions	Some Deficiency Symptoms	Some Overconsumption Symptoms
Functions as part of a coenzyme in fat synthesis, tissue respiration, and utilization of carbohydrate for energy. Promotes healthy skin, nerves, and digestive tract. Aids digestion and fosters normal appetite.	Skin and gastrointestinal lesions, anorexia, weakness, irritability, vertigo. *Severe:* pellagra.	None reported for nicotinamide. Flushing, headache, cramps, nausea for nicotinic acid.
Functions as part of coenzymes in amino acid and nucleoprotein metabolism. Promotes red blood cell formation.	Red tongue, diarrhea, anemia.	May obscure the existence of pernicious anemia.
Functions as part of a coenzyme involved in protein metabolism, assists in conversion of tryptophan to niacin, fatty acid metabolism, and red blood cell formation.	Irritability, muscle twitching, dermatitis near eyes, kidney stones, hypochromic anemia.	None reported.
Functions in coenzymes involved in nucleic acid synthesis and biological methylation. Assists in development of normal red blood cells and maintenance of nerve tissue.	*Severe:* pernicious anemia, neurological disorders.	None reported.

Appendix E: Some Healthy Reading

Every week, I get phone calls and questions regarding the names of recommended books on both general and sports nutrition. Following is a list of books I think you may find helpful and interesting.

COOKBOOKS

The American Heart Association Cookbook
Ruthe Eshleman and Mary Winston
David McKay, Inc., 1979.

> A popular cookbook containing over 550 tested recipes for those concerned about their calorie, fat, and cholesterol intake. It also provides excellent information on nutrition and heart disease.

Diet for a Small Planet
Frances More Lappe
Ballantine Books, 1980.

> An excellent resource for learning to combine proteins for a meatless vegetarian diet.

Laurel's Kitchen: A Handbook for Vegetarian Nutrition and Cookery
Laurel Robertson, Carol Flinders, and Bronwen Godfrey
Nilgiri Press, Berkeley, CA, 1978.

> Recipes and menus in addition to basic
> principles of nutrition applied to a vegetarian
> diet.

GENERAL NUTRITION

A Diet for Living
Jean Mayer
David McKay, Inc., NY, 1975.

> Answers to some commonly asked nutrition
> questions, including weight control, consumer
> issues, and heart disease.

The Family Guide to Better Food and Better Health
Ronald Deutsch
Creative Home Library, Des Moines, IA, 1971.

> A well-written, informative book, covering all
> aspects of nutrition for each member of the
> family.

Eating Your Way Through Life
Judith Wurtman
Raven Press, NY, 1979.

> A common-sense approach to eating, growing,
> and dieting, including consumer issues and
> practical nutrition information.

SPORTS NUTRITION

A Scientific Approach to Running
David Costill
Track and Field News, 1979.

> An exercise physiologist's detailed look at
> nutritional and other factors affecting training
> and endurance exercise.

Nutrition, Weight Control, and Exercise
Frank Katch and William McArdle
Houghton Mifflin Co., MA, 1977.

> A textbook approach to nutrition, exercise,
> caloric expenditure, and training.

WEIGHT CONTROL

Eating is OK! A radical approach to successful weight loss
Henry Jordan
Signet, NY, 1977.

> This book helps the reader to identify and
> change eating patterns that lead to obesity and
> to learn new, weight-conscious eating habits.

VITAMINS

The Vitamin Book
Editors of Consumer Guide
Simon & Schuster, 1979.

> A comprehensive, easy to understand look at
> vitamins, their functions, daily requirements,
> and food sources.

ADDITIVES

Eater's Digest—The Consumer's Factbook of Food Additives
Michael Jacobson
Doubleday and Co., Inc., NY, 1976.

> This book steers a sensible course between the natural food fanatics and the food industry.

FOOD COMPOSITION

Calories and Carbohydrates
Barbara Kraus
Signet, 1979.

> A listing of over 8,000 brand name and basic foods with their caloric and carbohydrate content.

Bowes and Church's Food Values of Portions Commonly Used
J. Pennington and H. N. Church
Harper and Row, Publishers, 1980.

> A comprehensive listing of foods, giving the value of 16 nutrients and 8 amino acids per serving.

Selected Bibliography

1. Bergstrom, J., I. Hermansen, E. Hultman, and B. Saltin. "Diet, Muscle Glycogen and Physical Performance." *Acta Physiol. Scand.* 71:140, 1967.

2. Costill, D., R. Bowers, G. Branam, and K. Sparks. "Muscle Glycogen Utilization during Prolonged Exercise on Successive Days." *J. Appl. Physiol.* 31:834, 1971.

3. Costill, D., E. Coyle, G. Dalsky, W. Evans, W. Fink, and D. Hoopes.
"Effect of Elevated Plasma FFA and Insulin on Muscle Glycogen Usage During Exercise." *J. Appl. Physiol.* 43:695, 1977.

4. Costill, D., G. Dalsky, and W. Fink.
"Effects of Caffeine Ingestion on Metabolism and Exercise Performance." *Med. Sci. Sports* 10:155, 1978.

5. Costill, D. and B. Saltin.
"Factors Limiting Gastric Emptying During Exercise and Rest." *J. Appl. Physiol.* 37:697, 1974.

6. Ehn, L., B. Carlmarsh, and S. Hoglund.
"Iron Status in Athletes Involved in Intense Physical Activity." *Med. Sci. Sports* 12:61, 1980.

7. Evans, W., A. Bennet, D. Costill, and W. Fink.
"Leg Muscle Metabolism in Trained and Untrained Men." *Res. Quart.* 50:350, 1979.

8. Ivy, J., D. Costill, W. Fink, and R. Lower.
"Influence of Caffeine and Carbohydrate Feedings on Endurance Performance." *Med. Sci. Sports* 11:6, 1979.

Index

ABOUT THE AUTHOR

Nancy Clark is a registered dietitian with additional training in exercise physiology. Currently she is the sports nutritionist for Sports Medicine Resource, Inc. in Boston, Massachusetts. She counsels both professional and recreational athletes regarding ways to optimize their diets. Ms. Clark also lectures at schools, colleges, and sports medicine conferences. She frequently appears on television and radio, and is the author of many sports nutrition articles.

BANTAM
SHOP·AT·HOME
C·A·T·A·L·O·G

Special Offer
Buy a Bantam Book
for only 50¢.

Now you can have Bantam's catalog filled with hundreds of titles plus take advantage of our unique and exciting bonus book offer. A special offer which gives you the opportunity to purchase a Bantam book for only 50¢. Here's how!

By ordering any five books at the regular price per order, you can also choose any other single book listed (up to a $4.95 value) for just 50¢. Some restrictions do apply, but for further details why not send for Bantam's catalog of titles today!

Just send us your name and address and we will send you a catalog!